NEW OXFORD ENGLISH SERIES

General Editor: A. NORMAN JEFFARES

SPENSER

SELECTIONS FROM THE MINOR POEMS AND *THE FAERIE QUEENE*

chosen and edited by

 FRANK KERMODE

JOHN EDWARD TAYLOR PROFESSOR OF ENGLISH LITERATURE
UNIVERSITY OF MANCHESTER

OXFORD UNIVERSITY PRESS

1965

Oxford University Press, Amen House, London E.C.4

GLASGOW NEW YORK TORONTO MELBOURNE WELLINGTON
BOMBAY CALCUTTA MADRAS KARACHI LAHORE DACCA
CAPE TOWN SALISBURY NAIROBI IBADAN ACCRA
KUALA LUMPUR HONG KONG

Cover portrait by Leonard Rosoman

Printed in Great Britain by
The Camelot Press Ltd., London and Southampton

CONTENTS

INTRODUCTION

IN making this selection of the poetry of Spenser I have tried to present him in such a way as to encourage modern readers to take an interest in a great poet who has for too long been neglected by all save scholars and a small band of private enthusiasts. To do so requires a somewhat unconventional approach. Spenser is important to the modern reader not as the maker of neologisms; nor as the man who so freely (and sometimes, as editors like to point out, inaccurately) alluded to classical myths and classical authors; nor even as the poet who was acknowledged as the greatest of his time by his contemporaries, and as the master of his trade. This kind of importance is perfectly consistent with a tendency to bore an audience three hundred and seventy years on. And if an editor believes, as I do, that Spenser is not only capable of but demands such an interest, his task is not merely to mention some of the known facts, to explain allusions to classical myths and authors, and to such contemporaries as Sidney, Essex, Raleigh, Lord Grey and the Queen, and to gloss the hard words. He must somehow make it credible that Spenser is a poet of extraordinary power, of manifold and interesting contradictions. He must show that *The Faerie Queene* can be called 'dreamy' only if we allow that dreams have urgent meanings, and that Spenser's 'gentleness', his soft beauty and his slow pace, are paradoxically consistent with great imaginative strength, and with an unusually powerful grasp of the actual.

Hence he must undertake the important general rather than the trifling particular explanation. The whole of the poem is not to be got into a book of this size, but it is essential that its scope should be felt. Consequently the notes to this book are made up only partly of glosses to words and names; each extract is prefaced by a long note relating it to the whole book in which it occurs, and attempting a brief and simple account of the meaning and design of each book. This introduction provides a slender account of Spenser's life and work, and, in its last part, speaks more generally of the poetry than the notes can do.

Spenser was born in London, perhaps in East Smithfield, in 1552, or within the two years following. He was related to a noble Spencer family, but was not himself richly born. From 1561 he attended a famous Elizabethan school, Merchant Taylors, then a new foundation, and, under the eye of the great schoolmaster Richard Mulcaster, he led for eight years the arduous life of an Elizabethan schoolboy. He would learn, probably, a little Hebrew, some Greek, and a great deal of Latin; but Mulcaster also included English in his syllabus, as well as singing and acting. Spenser was a 'poore scholler' and paid no fees, thought his does not mean that his family was destitute.

In 1569, he obtained a grant from a charitable fund and matriculated at Pembroke Hall, Cambridge, as a sizar (poor student). This required him to do certain jobs around the college in return for free meals, but did not limit his right to enjoy the benefits available at this militantly Puritan college. He would study rhetoric, logic and moral philosophy, and take part in formal exercises in disputation. After four years (the *quadrivium*) he graduated B.A., and embarked on the *trivium*, the three-year M.A. course, which included philosophy, astronomy, Greek, and mathematics. Most of this study was based on ancient authors. There was no formal study of modern languages.

Spenser was already a poet when he arrived in Cambridge: he had published in 1569 translations of Du Bellay and Petrarch in a book by John Vandernoodt called *The Theatre of Voluptuous Worldlings*. Cambridge could undoubtedly provide him with the learning considered essential to poetry, and stimulate his interest in those pressing theological controversies which were to leave their mark on his later work. But his direct interest in poetry was also nourished, largely by his friendship with Gabriel Harvey. Harvey, a Fellow of Pembroke from 1570, was the son of a farmer from Saffron Walden, and a man at once learned and likable, pedantic and vain. The friendship he formed with Spenser was never broken, but he was much disliked by others, and later became famous for his acrimonious pamphlet exchanges with Nashe; perhaps Shakespeare ridiculed him as the pedant in *Love's Labour's Lost*.

One of Harvey's interests was English versification. He wanted to introduce into the language the quantitative prosody of Latin. Of this and other projects we read in an exchange of letters with Spenser; they were published in 1580. Spenser sent Harvey some experiments, and requested fuller instructions in the art, which, he adds, was also the concern of Sir Philip Sidney and others in his circle. He speaks of more elaborate instances of 'Englishe Versifying' that he has in hand. Harvey complies, but, more interestingly, mentions by name a list of works by Spenser, complete, in process of writing, or projected. They amount to a large body of work, none of which survives. He gossips, too, about Cambridge and fashions in learning there; but the passage that time has made most important is that in which he speaks slightingly of *The Faerie Queene*. Some part of it, then, he had seen in 1580, but he writes that he prefers the *Nine Comedies* (one for each Muse) of Spenser; they come

nearer Ariosto's comedies, he says, than *The Faerie Queene*
approaches the *Orlando Furioso* of the same author, 'which
not withstanding, you wil needes seeme to emulate, and hope
to overgo, as you flatly professed. . . .' And he hopes that if
Spenser disagrees, 'God or some good Aungell' will put him
in a better mind. It is curious that in this same letter Harvey
mentions the opinion of a divine that St. John's Revelation was
to be preferred over all visionary poetry as the 'moste wonder-
full Propheticall, or Poetical Vision', but that Spenser will
doubtless be satisfied with something inferior, like *The Faerie
Queene*. This suggests that the part Harvey saw was not Book I,
but probably something now embedded in III or IV, if it survives at all; for Book I is not Ariostan, and is largely based
on Revelation. Replying, Spenser speaks of the Areopagus, a
group consisting of himself, Sidney, and Dyer, and dedicated
to the purgation of English rhyming; but what we see clearly
is that Spenser, whose beginnings in poetry are so closely
associated with Harvey, had by this time firmly established
himself in the English tradition, and will meddle no more
with radical classical 'reforms'.

These letters were, of course, written after Spenser had left
Cambridge, and when he had behind him the highly experimental, but not quantitative, verse of the *Shepheardes Calender*.
After graduating M.A. in 1576, he had visited his kinsmen
in Lancashire. There he seems to have met Rosalind, a girl
about whom Harvey teases him, and who has an important
place in the *Calender* and in *Colin Clouts Come Home Againe*.
In 1577 he perhaps made his first trip to Ireland; certainly in
the following year he was in London, secretary to John
Young, bishop of Rochester, who had been Master of Pembroke—one of the good bishops of the *Calender*. Soon he
was in the service of the powerful Earl of Leicester; hence his
acquaintance with Leicester's nephew Sidney. In 1579 he

married Machabyas Childe, and published the *Calender*, with a dedication to Sidney which, as we see from a letter to Harvey, he was hesitant about risking. Sidney admired it, with reservations which are explained in the *Defence of Poesie*,[1] and it was soon, as Harvey said, a 'famous' poem, the foundation of the extraordinary development of English poetry in the second half of Elizabeth's reign. Spenser was now familiar with the court, and began the bold satire *Mother Hubberds Tale*, a beast fable with strong political implications; Spenser was of the party which disliked Burghley and opposed the projected marriage of the Queen to Alençon. But as we have seen, he was already by 1580 at work on *The Faerie Queene*; imitating Virgil, he progressed from pastoral to epic.

In 1580 he became secretary to Lord Grey de Wilton, recently appointed Lord Deputy of Ireland; and save for some visits to London he spent the rest of his life in that country. The story of English rule in Ireland is continuously wretched, and Elizabeth's part in it is not among the happier aspects of her reign. Ireland was virtually a colony, and the first duty of the colonist, old- or new-world, was to make a profit. Elizabeth's planter-poet arrived to find two other groups—the Irish themselves, poor, Catholic, mutinous, and the Anglo-Irish, who had been there for so long that they were almost a native ruling class. The new men got on with neither; they wanted to impose Protestant religion, English justice, and agricultural schemes suitable to their own profit, on an unwilling nation. The troubles that ensued it was for years the business of Lord Grey to suppress, and he did so with notorious severity. Spenser thoroughly approved, as we gather from many comments, as in *The Faerie Queene* V,

[1] Spenser 'hath much Poetrie in his Eglogues. . . . That same framing of his stile to an old rustick language I dare not alowe. . . .'

but most explicitly in the posthumous prose work, *A Vewe of the Present State of Irelande*, written about 1596.

Spenser presumably lived in Dublin Castle at first, but already by 1582 he had rented a house near Dublin, as if intending a long stay. But he also, it seems, accompanied Grey on the military expeditions by which he implemented his severe policies of pacification, endorsed by Spenser in the *Vewe*. He may well have seen Grey in action as Justice, with his troops in the role of Talus (the impersonal agent of Justice in *Faerie Queene* V); but London was uneasy in its support of Grey, and sometimes favoured conciliation. Conscious of inadequate backing, Grey sought to be relieved of his post. After a good deal of ill-feeling and backbiting, as if by the Blatant Beast, he returned home in 1582.

Spenser, though much involved in his secretaryship and its rewards, made another literary friend at about this time, with the result that one more document relating to the pre-history of *The Faerie Queene* has survived. The friend was Lodowick Bryskett, another civil servant in Ireland, something of a poet and acquainted with Sidney. His book called *A Discourse of Civil Life, Containing the Ethic Part of Moral Philosophy*, published in 1606, is largely based on an Italian work about the education of a gentleman by the scholar-poet Cinthio; but in it he describes conversations, perhaps imaginary, between himself, Spenser, and other gentlemen at his cottage near Dublin. Spenser, asked to discourse on moral philosophy and particularly on the virtues, excuses himself on the ground that he has a poem in hand on this very subject —'in *heroical verse* under the title of a *Faerie Queene* . . . assigning to every vertue a Knight to be the patron and defender of the same'. We can be reasonably sure, even allowing for hindsight on Bryskett's part, that Spenser was at work on the poem, and that he may by now have settled on its general design; for, as I have noted, Harvey's earlier words suggests that he had begun with a much more Ariostan poem than Books I and II turned out to be, and it has been conjectured that the first parts to be written belonged to Books III and IV.[1]

Spenser made other literary friends—notably the poets Googe and Rich—and continued in the Government service. From 1588 his work and his residence were in Munster; in that year he acquired his estate at Kilcolman, between Limerick and Cork. This was a 3,000-acre grant in a beautiful but depopulated countryside, and adjacent to larger estates granted to Raleigh and Sir Christopher Hatton. He established six English farmers on his land. Spenser was now a man of some substance, suffering no qualms at the exploitation of the Irish—for that was not the mood of Elizabethan colonists— and enjoying his countryside; the environs of Kilcolman are frequently celebrated and mythologized in *The Faerie Queene*.

In 1589 his neighbour Raleigh came over to visit his own estate, and called on Spenser. Spenser showed him the big poem, and Raleigh induced the poet to return with him to London. The Queen liked the first three books; in 1590 they were published. Spenser's reward was a pension of £50, a sum which, though not inconsiderable, disappointed him. He never got on with Burghley, nor did Raleigh; and some of his disappointment is reflected in *Colin Clouts Come Home Againe* as well as in the proem to Book IV. But the book enjoyed much success, and in the following year Spenser, after his return to Ireland, published several poems—the *Complaints*, consisting of *Muiopotmos*, *Mother Hubberds Tale*, *Daphnaida* and others—to take advantage of it.

[1] For a very elaborate conjecture as to the order of composition and changes of purpose, see J. W. Bennett, *The Evolution of The Faerie Queene*, Chicago, (1942).

In Ireland he was involved in difficult and laborious law-suits, but his literary activity must have been almost continuous. If the attribution is correct, he translated the pseudo-Platonic dialogue *Axiochus*, published in 1592. His courtship of Elizabeth Boyle, and his second marriage[1] in 1594, are reflected in the *Amoretti*, a sonnet-sequence written presumably between 1591 and 1594, and the *Epithalamion* of 1595. In that year also he published *Colin Clouts Come Home Againe* and his elegy for Sidney. Meanwhile he had finished Books IV–VI of *The Faerie Queene*, though some parts of this may already have been written before the publication of I–III in 1590. In 1595 he took the new books to London and in the following year they were published, together with a second edition of I–III, by Richard Field, a Stratford man and an acquaintance of Shakespeare's. His interest in contemporary affairs was never greater than now, and he inserted a new passage in V. xi showing Arthegall as champion of Henri IV of France—an allusion presumably, to Essex and his championship of the Bourbon, or perhaps even to Sir John Norris, on whom had fallen Grey's task of pacifying Ireland. And he was writing his *Vewe of the Present State* of that country. Late in the year James VI of Scotland demanded Spenser's punishment for libelling his mother Mary Queen of Scots, who appears as Duessa in Book V; but no action was taken. Other works of this period included *The Fowre Hymns* and *Prothalamion*. The latter was written in honour of the double marriage of the daughters of the Earl of Worcester, a friend of Essex; the marriage was celebrated at Essex House where Spenser had been received into the service of Leicester nearly twenty years earlier. The *Hymns* are something of a problem, since Spenser says he wrote the first pair (to Love and to Beauty) in his youth, claiming that the second pair (to

[1] Nobody knows what became of the first Mrs. Spenser.

Heavenly Love and Heavenly Beauty), which are more Christian, belong to his maturer years, and should be read as amendments or retractations of the earlier. It seems doubtful whether this can be so; the less explicitly Christian Platonism of the first two is not fundamentally inconsistent with the theology of the last two, and they are complementary in a way familiar to students of *The Faerie Queene*. Perhaps they were all written over the same period of time, late rather than early.[1]

Spenser's distaste for court life is reflected in *Prothalamion*, and in many places in the later books of the epic. To his disappointment the continuation of the poem brought him no reward, though Book V might have been expected to please the Queen almost as much as Book I. He went back to Ireland, probably late in 1596. This time his stay there was shorter. He was appointed Sheriff of Cork in 1598, but soon the much-feared rebellion of Tyrone broke out. Tyrone was later to help bring down Essex; now he accomplished the ruin of a lesser political figure, Spenser. Kilcolman was sacked, and Spenser fled to Cork; from there he carried dispatches to the Privy Council in London at the end of 1598. A month later, on 16 January 1599, he died, probably not, as Jonson told Drummond, 'for lack of bred', for he had his pension at least. Essex paid for his funeral in Westminster Abbey, where he was buried near Chaucer; and poets threw elegies into the grave. The Queen seems to have ordered a monument, but it was not erected; and in 1620 Anne Clifford, Countess of Dorset, provided one, which got the dates of birth and death wrong, but contained the famous eulogy, 'The Prince of Poets in his Tyme.' It was restored in marble in 1778, with the dates corrected, and may be seen in Poets' Corner.

---

[1] R. Ellrodt, *Neoplatonism in the Poetry of Spenser*, makes an important issue of their date; his is the best modern study of Spenser's Platonism.

It is risky to say much about the personal character of a
man on the strength of such information as we possess concerning Spenser.[1] He was scholarly, though not perhaps
extremely learned—his was a poet's scholarship, and might
be called, in Harvey's phrase, 'curious and universal' without
being minute. He was ambitious, and, despite the frustration
of many of his courtly aspirations, he had a successful career
in the world. His ambitions were double, and called for
exceptional industry; evidently he was a diligent secretary,
and certainly he practised his poetry—from which he sought
not only glory but material reward—with an industry almost
as remarkable as his skill. He was a literary adventurer, seeking in the past models for entirely original achievement, as
the voyagers did. Indeed he was, like many great men of the
time, a blend of apparent opposites. His views on Ireland
seem cruel, yet he was gentle. He had fierce views on the
subjection of women, as Book V shows; yet he may have
broken off the composition of that book to write *Epithalamion*, and most of his life-work is an act of worship offered to
a woman. He was oppressed by signs of returning chaos in
the world, but often celebrated love as an inexhaustible
source of beauty and order. He was deeply committed to
foreign poetry, yet, like his Queen, he was 'mere English'.
He was the poet of order, of complex organization, of courtesy; yet he supported the war party and the ruthless solution.
Spenser's great poem, as we shall see, is built on radical
oppositions, philosophically and poetically considered. His
life, perhaps, reflected the same antinomies.

Even so brief an account of Spenser's life makes clear two
important facts. He hoped by poetry to achieve worldly

[1] The standard biography is that of A. C. Judson contained in the American
Variorum edition of *The Works of Spenser* (vol. II, Baltimore, 1945).

success (and to a considerable extent succeeded, though not as he had hoped). Secondly, the way he went about this brought him into contact with the great ones of the age to a degree that might astonish a poet of our time; and the knowledge and service of great men required that one stand close also to the great events and policies with which they were concerned. The quest for patronage in Elizabethan England was more often disappointed than not, and involved some time-serving;[1] yet it was mostly beneficial, and obviously directed Spenser from the beginning of his mature poetry to that interest in the actual, in history and politics, which so strikingly colours his dream-poetry.

Among the great men Spenser certainly, if humbly, knew, were Leicester and his nephew Sidney, Essex, and Raleigh. The names alone are sufficient to conjure up ideas of the great Elizabethan expansion, the aspect of Elizabethan England we all think of first. Spenser thought of them, too. He wrote of the age of discovery, of the 'hardy enterprize' through which 'many great regions are discovered'; of him who 'in venturous vessell measured/The Amazons huge river'. It seemed to him that the 'Elizabethan Settlement' had restored some stability

[1] For the fuller accounts of this interesting subject, see E. H. Miller, *The Professional Writer*, Cambridge, Mass. (1959) and J. Buxton, *Sidney and the English Renaissance*, London and Toronto (1954). There is a briefer study in *Shakespeare's England*, New York and London (1916) and an excellent brief article about Spenser, Harvey and their quest for patronage in M. C. Bradbrook's 'No Room at the Top', *Elizabethan Poetry*, ed. Brown and Harris (Stratford-upon-Avon Studies 2), London, 1960, pp. 90–109. Publication was a delicate business because of the convention that gentlemen did not do it. Elizabeth generally left the rewarding of poets to her courtiers, and of these Sidney and his sister were much the most enlightened and generous. But Spenser made a disastrous mistake in taking Sidney's line on the proposed Alençon marriage and writing *Mother Hubberds Tale*. This won him the dislike of Burghley, who favoured the match; the failure of his hopes in Leicester and the enmity of the most powerful man of all ensured the disappointment of his highest hopes.

to a tormented nation, and that the Queen who, with all her faults, brought power and intellect to the handling of the vast problems of her long reign, deserved the adulation she demanded. Though he envied and imitated the achievements of the earlier-flowering European renaissances, he rejoiced in the lengthening tradition of English humanist learning. Not only the conceited daring of Raleigh but the absolute courtiership and fire of Sidney and the princely power of Essex were to him indications of a reborn imperial splendour; and like any celebrant of national power he sought its origins in a glorious British past. He accepted the religious settlement as good, and worthy to be preserved and defended; he rejoiced in the metropolitan splendours of a growing London; he cherished the native language, and also the nation's military power, which Elizabeth, however, used more cautiously than some of Spenser's friends would have liked. To this extent Spenser knew and admired an Elizabethan England of the sort we all hear about at school.

But Elizabethan England was neither so happy nor so emancipated from the Middle Ages as the conventional picture suggests. The imperialism of the age was the descendant of medieval 'universalism', but it was also the ancestor of modern nationalism. If 1559 is an important date, because then the Acts of Supremacy and Uniformity gave the country a foundation of peace and order, so is 1558; Calais was lost, and that marks a sharper and narrower nationalism, a cleaner separation of England from Europe. Throughout her reign Elizabeth was called Queen of France and of Ireland; but the first title was a formality, and the second a matter of endless contention, which was to darken still more the last years of the reign. England certainly became the chief power of Protestant Europe, but this involved Elizabeth in the long and mostly cold war with Spain. When we think of the great literary achievements of the reign we see its closing years as especially glorious, but they were also years of inexplicably rising prices and social unrest—the first great slump in our history, in the first age of capitalism.

Nor had the earlier part of the reign been without intractable problems. All the evidence is consistent with the view that Elizabeth was a great woman, probably the best equipped monarch in our history.[1] But the difficulties she inherited, and some she created, were enormous. There was the permanent and delicate issue of the succession, which grew worse when the Queen passed the age of child-bearing without marrying; and this was the problem she could least endure to have discussed. Involved with the religious question, it was, for example, responsible for the 1570 rebellion of the Northern earls, supporters of Mary Queen of Scots. Elizabeth's last marriage project, and the visit of Simier and Alençon in 1579, deeply divided her counsellors; 'these wooing matters', as Walsingham called them, set Burghley against Spenser's noble friends, and cost the Puritan writer Stubbs his right hand. With the breakdown of the courtship there disappeared the last faint chance of a Tudor heir. For its last twenty-three years, the reign was under the cloud of strong Stuart claims to the succession. Mary Stuart was executed in 1587; in the following year Elizabeth, as usual desperate for money, had to prepare for the naval onslaught of her Spanish brother-in-law, and for the rising of English Catholics which would receive him. Amid the rejoicing at the defeat of the Armada, Leicester, whom, years before, she would have liked to marry, died. The favourite of the closing years was the brilliant Essex; and Essex was executed in 1601 after the strangest of all rebellions, the purpose of which was again to determine

[1] The best biography is J. E. Neale, *Queen Elizabeth*, New York, Toronto and London (1934).

Bs

the problem of the succession by gaining power and openly declaring for James VI of Scotland, son of Mary Stuart.

Spenser we associate with the cult of Elizabeth's virginity, which was carried to such extraordinary heights of chivalric poetry. It must not be dismissed as disingenuous time-serving, but it was certainly a way, originally, of making the best of a bad situation. And Spenser, even after his removal to Ireland cut him off from day-to-day developments, had a lasting concern for this and for all the inextricably interlinked problems of the reign. Elizabeth's long, unequal duel with Mary Stuart was an aspect of her foreign policy; hence there is nothing strange about Spenser's sending Arthur from the trial of Duessa (Mary) to the fighting in the Netherlands, or about Arthegall's support for Henri IV. Even the Irish problem, so dominant in Book V, was associated with the conflict between the great Catholic and Protestant powers. And throughout his life Spenser was deeply interested in the religious problems which were reflected in all the strife, internal and foreign, of Elizabeth's reign,

These religious problems were of daunting complexity, and, as I suggested above, they had many implications in every sphere of the nation's life. Many people, when Elizabeth succeeded to the throne in 1558, had lived through her father's dispute with Rome, through the brief period of triumphant Protestantism under Edward VI, and through the Catholic reaction under Mary Tudor. Elizabeth was herself far from extreme Protestantism, and her settlement of 1559 had all the disadvantages of compromise: for years it pleased neither Catholic nor Protestant. The Church now established claimed to be both; a Catholic church purged by Protestant action, with the monarch as its supreme governor. Conformity was required, and recusancy punished by law. Elizabeth's first clergy was largely made up of priests who had varied their doctrines with each new reign. They were rarely learned and usually underpaid. Her bishops were undistinguished, certainly as apologists of the new settlement, and they were often venal; in their turn they were exploited by the great laymen who had profited by the Reformation dissolutions. The Church had arrived at a position where only a remarkable effort of ecclesiastical intelligence could save it; and it was vulnerable to attack from Protestant and Catholic alike.

All these contingencies occurred. The apologia was forthcoming. Foxe provided a version of ecclesiastical history, Jewel a learned apology for the Anglican position, Archbishop Parker a suitable history of the English Church, and, climactic achievement, Hooker justified the Church of the middle way in the broadest historical and theological terms. And to this Church—older than Rome, subject to an empress who had inherited the powers of Constantine, originally founded directly after the crucifixion by Joseph of Arimathea—Spenser gave his allegiance. His history is that of Foxe, Jewel, and Parker; his faith is roughly that of the Prayer Book Articles as we still have them. He was well aware of the corruptions and doctrinal muddles that abounded, and the *Shepheardes Calender* is full of comment on contemporary bishops, good and bad. But the Settlement became for him a type, as it were, of Eden, a marriage of Una with Red Cross, of the one true faith with England. He is the poet of the first Anglicanism.

Nevertheless, he was concerned, as everybody must have been, with contemporary dissent, Puritan and Catholic. The Puritan criticism of the Settlement—that it preserved gross elements of popery—reached its first peak in Cambridge while Spenser was a student, with the expulsion of Cartwright, the Puritan leader, from the Chair of Divinity. Broadly speaking the Puritans, though they also had many ceremonial objections to the established Church, were most deeply disturbed by the power of the bishops, for which they saw no scriptural warrant; in short, they were Presbyterians. They also opposed the survival of Romanist liturgy in the Prayer Book. Although their opposition was at first stated from within the Church, the controversy grew open and bitter. Spenser's friend Harvey was involved. With many of the complaints of corruption and calls for reform Spenser must certainly have sympathized; but he was never a Puritan,[1] and always, and increasingly, a supporter of the Settlement.

The problem of the Puritans, despite the links with continental reformers, was, though serious, largely domestic. The Catholic problem was a matter of national security. Obviously there were great numbers of Englishmen who remained, more or less secretly, loyal to the old faith, and there were some who paid heavy fines for recusancy (including, perhaps, John Shakespeare). But the strength of Catholic feeling grew to be alarming only when the Jesuit missionaries, a formidable body of men trained to persist till death, began to arrive from Douai in the late seventies. Pius V had excommunicated Elizabeth at the time of the Northern Rebellion in 1570, and the papacy was involved in plots against her throne and her life. So the Jesuit missionaries were hunted with great cruelty, and what with this struggle and the Catholic plots, civil hatred combined with the Spanish threat to make religion a singularly grim issue. Elizabeth's diplomacy and her (remarkably few) military adventures were all related to the Catholic threat, and Spenser is not alone in calling the papacy antichrist, and the Roman Church a type of perfidy and

[1] The best study of Spenser's doctrinal position is V. K. Whitaker, *The Religious Basis of Spenser's Poetry*, Stanford (1950). A concise account of his attitude to ecclesiastical problems at the time of writing *Shepheardes Calender* is P. E. McLane's book (see Select Bibliography), especially Chapter VII.

duplicity. His Archimago is the papacy, even individual popes—especially the two most hated, Sylvester II and Gregory VII, who were not only associated with a great increase in papal authority but had passed into Protestant tradition as magicians and devil-worshippers.

It is at this point that we may see how Spenser as a poet made a myth of the historical situation. *The Faerie Queene* is by no means lacking in criticism of the English attitude to true religion; but Book I represents the Church of England as the one true primitive catholic church, and the Church of Rome as deviant and heretical. Spenser, making Truth the Church of England and Falsehood the Church of Rome, is writing poetry out of what he really believed: that in principle the reformed Church of England was the true primitive church, long lost in the wilderness and now, by his empress, restored.

It is characteristic of Spenser that he represented this as an imperfect restoration. In the same way, he saw the England of Elizabeth as glorious, and her court as the fount of courtesy, but still thought of the nation as subject to evil and decay, and the court as ungrateful and containing corruption. He would undoubtedly have endorsed Milton's bold phrase, 'God's Englishmen'; but this view, that his countrymen had attained a special place in God's plans for what was left of time, did not seem incompatible with the opinion that the world was in visible decay, and that the remnant of time was also in some ways the dregs of time.

This polarity of light and dark is essential to his mind. Whether or no he was versed in Renaissance Platonism,[1] one can certainly call Spenser a Christian Platonist and he

[1] Professor Ellrodt, op. cit., (see Bibliography) thinks he was not, except in the *Fowre Hymns*, all of which he regards as late.

had the kind of mind which can take intense pleasure in the forms, colours, and movement of life while acknowledging that all created things had shared in the Fall, and confessing their inferiority to the white ideal stillness of eternity. His *Muiopotmos* is probably an allegory of the descent of the soul into matter, a Platonic theme; the little epyllion—if we may call it by the name given in Alexandria to the brief mythological epic—is light enough in spirit, but it enacts the tragedy of the Fall. The Garden of Adonis in Book III is as delightful in its celebration of fertility and generation as *Epithalamion*; but it is 'fleshly slime' that Genius provides for the souls to inhabit. Life is colour and form, but it is also trial and initiation; the Bower of Bliss is bad, the House of Celia, with its stringent corrections, good. Mammon's Cave is the temple of world, flesh, and devil. The Mutabilitie Cantos delight in the huge variety of times and seasons, but time is still the drudge of eternity. The various and mutable, in which the senses delight, belongs to a lower sphere than the changeless and eternal, which the higher powers of the mind may contemplate.

This polarity is expressed in some of Spenser's imagery: the armour of Red Cross in the first canto makes, in the den of Error, 'a little glooming light, much like a shade'; in the last canto of the same book Una at last lays 'her mournefull stole aside' and we see 'The blazing brightnesse of her beauties beame,/And glorious light of her sunshyny face.' Arthur's address to Night at the end of III. iv is one of the richest passages in the poem; Night conceals the beauty of the creation and is the interval of death between two different experiences of light. Spenser's mind moves like a tide between the shores of light and darkness, as between the other great opposites, life and death, the changing and the changeless, time and eternity.

This movement, the great slow swing of Spenser's mind, cannot be felt in the shorter poems as fully as in the huge expanse of the epic. And that was the task for which he consciously prepared himself. It is commonplace that he was, in a sense, at a new beginning of English poetry, and that he looked back, for his only possible English exemplar, to Chaucer. He also felt (and studied in French poetry) the Renaissance need to dignify and strengthen the 'vulgar' national language. *The Shepheardes Calender* is experimental in diction, not only because pastoral calls for a 'Doric' or rustic accent, but because Spenser and his friends, at Cambridge and at court, saw that if there was to be a new English poetry there must be experiment. And the way for an epic poet to begin, as Virgil's supreme example showed, was to write pastoral.

As we know from the Harvey correspondence, Spenser had, by 1580, written a great deal; much of it is lost, though some of it may be incorporated in *The Faerie Queene*. He needed practice and experiment in many kinds—pastoral, satire, epyllion, complaint. Unlike Sidney, he seems not to have experimented extensively in quantitative metres, but he nevertheless made a wide range of prosodic experiments in the *Calender*, not all of them pleasing, but all exploratory. If you think of a young poet today, writing *vers libre* and syllabic verse as well as more regular iambic forms, and perhaps ballads, you get some notion of what occupied him, though of course he had not behind him, as the modern poet has, a long and much-studied English tradition.

Yet it would be very misleading to think of him as standing quite free of the past; no poet can do that. The comments of E. K. on *The Shepheardes Calender* (and I agree with M. C. Bradbrook that Harvey is the most likely author) delights in the traditional rhetorical devices of the eclogues, and Spenser, like all other Elizabethan poets, used them as his education

dictated, namely as modes of persuasion and communication
tried by time and incumbent on all whose aim was, as his
must be, to persuade men through delight to virtue.[1] Nor
should we underestimate the common stock of philosophy
and studies in ancient authors which Spenser by education
shared with his contemporaries; or neglect the truth that for
all the humanist changes that had affected it, this education
was much more 'medieval' in character than we often sup-
pose. There are in Spenser elements, for instance of philosophy
and theology, which can seem to us strangely learned, but
which would probably have passed unnoticed, so far as
scholarship goes, in educated company, not only in his day
but for centuries before it.

Now Spenser himself calls his great poem 'a continued
allegory', so there is a real need, in any introduction, to say a
word about the antecedents of this mode. First, it is by no
means inconsistent with a desire to emulate Virgil. Virgil
had been for centuries read as an allegorical poet, and his first
six books especially were a 'dark conceit' with hidden spiritual
meanings. The original opening of the *Aeneid*, in which Virgil
speaks of himself as the man who once wrote pastorals but
now emerges from the woods to sing of arms and the man,
is echoed in the opening lines of Spenser's Proem. Virgil's
moral purpose, which was held to be an education in the
virtues, is Spenser's. As Aeneas is the parent of Rome and the
type of Augustus Caesar, so Arthur (and other characters, such
as Britomart and Arthegall) are types and progenitors of the
new Britain under the Tudors. Virgil's other Renaissance
emulators, notably Tasso, had many of the same aims, including an intention to produce allegory. In Ariosto there are some
clearly allegorical passages; but allegory is not his principal

[1] For the subtleties of rhetoric in Elizabethan poetry, see Rosemond Tuve,
Elizabethan and Metaphysical Imagery, Chicago and London (1947).

mode. Tasso produced an allegorical reading of the *Gerusa-
lemme Liberata*, but it has the appearance of something that was
largely worked out later, rather than an intrinsic part of the
conception. Spenser borrowed a good deal from these two
poets (a famous example is Acrasia and her Bower) and in the
middle books he imitates the fragmentary romance narrative
of Ariosto closely; but for the most part his difference from
them can be summed up by saying that allegory was essential
to the operation of his imagination, as it was not to theirs.

We must not hamper ourselves with some narrow definition of the term 'allegory', or some sharp antithesis with
'symbolism'. Allegory is in Spenser an extremely various
mode, as it was and had been in England and throughout
Europe for centuries. Let us consider a few instances of the
practice of allegory, in order to illuminate Spenser's use of
it for the purposes outlined in the 'Letter to Raleigh' (on
which see Notes, pp. 185–188). To the medieval mind the
creation was a series of interrelated enigmas; 'embracing all
nature and history, symbolism gave a conception of the world,
of a still more rigorous unity than that which modern science
can offer'. So J. Huizinga, whose book *The Waning of the
Middle Ages*,[1] and especially the chapters 'Religious Thought
Crystallizing into Images', and 'Symbolism in its Decline',
with the others on love and chivalry, are an excellent introduction to this subject. Once the mind accepts that everything
is significant of truth, and assumes that the inter-relations
between all things have only to be discovered and asserted
to provide new knowledge of a higher reality, the way is
open to symbolic constructions of every kind, including
allegory that may vary from the simple to the mysterious.
There are symbolisms which seem gross, as in parts of the
House of Alma, or in the statue of the Virgin described by

[1] Published New York, 1924; Pelican edition 1955.

Huizinga: it had a stomach which opened to show the Trinity sitting inside, and was condemned not for its taste but for its theology. Yet symbolism could exercise a profound influence on high politics: Huizinga cites the influence on events of the medieval symbolism in which the sun stood for the Papacy, the Moon for the Empire, and the Two Swords for spiritual and temporal power.

This refers to an earlier period than Spenser's; but the tradition survived. There was poetry, the obscure philosophical allegories of Alanus, whom Spenser mentions in the Mutabilitie Cantos, or, nearer home, of Chaucer. There were the later allegorical poets, Gower, Hawes, and others. There was the long tradition of allegorical interpretation of ancient mythology, especially as it occurred in Ovid. There were, as C. S. Lewis properly insists in his history of allegory up to Spenser, the popular allegories, as in the morality plays, or the 'shows' of Spenser's period. From the morality plays one is familiar with that personification of mental or spiritual attributes which forms a staple of simple allegory. From the Lord-Mayor's-Show kind of entertainment one can see that Spenser's poem, for all its range and sophistication, has humble relatives. The great popular celebrations of the Queen's birthday included such shows; there might be a figure representing St. George, and a lady with a lamb. When the Queen's portrait was made, she was shown with symbols of virginity or empire. If she visited a great courtier on a progress, she would be met by reciters in allegorical costumes.[1] This was not a practice confined to one class. The City companies thought in allegory when they wished to make formal statements about their views of the City, the nation, or the

[1] For Queen's Day celebrations see Roy C. Strong 'The Popular Celebration of the Accession Day of Queen Elizabeth I', *Journal of the Warburg and Courtauld Institutes*, xxi (1958), pp. 86–103.

world. In the next reign the court masque celebrated royalty
or marriage in such subtle philosophical allegory that Jonson,
the greatest of the masque-writers, added deep footnotes
to the published text to provide justification and explanation
of his learned inventions. Yet there is a continuity between
the dark philosophical allegory and the commonplace allegories
of the street that permits us to speak, with C. S. Lewis, of
a 'homely, churchwardenly' Spenser, without abandoning
the right to think of him as a profound philosophical allegorist.

Huizinga speaks of a tendency, at the close of the Middle
Ages, to make 'an intellectual pastime' of symbolism and
allegory. This continued to be true, but who can say when the
game grows serious? A whole new development of the symbolic and allegorical modes in the Platonic academies of the
Renaissance had an incalculable effect on the tradition.[1]
Handbooks of symbolism, like those of Natalis Comes and
Cartari, proved indispensable to artists and poets (we know
that Spenser used Comes) and patrons could provide painters
with very elaborate Neo-Platonic 'programmes' of interlocking symbols (such as that from which Botticelli worked
when he painted the *Primavera*) that still defy the interpretative
skill of the scholar. *The Faerie Queene* is of its time, 'modern',
in that sense. Some of its allegory is simple, but it also contains elaborate programmatic allegories (constructed on a
provided scenario, the 'programmes' of Renaissance allegorical painters) which are deliberately 'dark'. What makes it
possible for them to live in the same poem as the simple
allegories is the continuing tradition described by Huizinga
—the assumption that, in one way or another, the world is
symbolic, and that men can see the symbols and read them;
but that the human mind can also arrive at truth by inventing

[1] See J. Seznec, *The Survival of the Pagan Gods*, London (1953) and E. Wind,
Pagan Mysteries in the Renaissance, London (1958).

new, or making new juxtapositions of old, symbols. If every simple story may yield a hidden significance to the acute reader, it is not surprising that poets can make fictions which embody hidden truth exactly in the manner of the old myths. Thus poetry can embody secret wisdom, and we must not be surprised to find, in the interwoven allegories of Spenser, many different *thicknesses* of meaning. Since the fabric is after all continuous, it is evident that even the simple parts are affected by the mysterious ones; the poem is not only complex but unfinished, and we shall never grasp anything like the whole of Spenser's intention. But if we are not prepared for the intellectual and imaginative exercise of this multiform allegory we shall grasp none of it.

Spenser establishes the fact that his poem is allegorical very early in the Letter to Raleigh, before proceeding to questions of ethical purpose, narrative and structure. He describes a plan for a Renaissance heroic poem: ethical, national, allegoric. To him it resembled Virgil's plan, allegory included; and he would not have thought that he was making any mystery more profound than that of the sixth book of the Aeneid. We can see wide differences between the methods of Virgil and Spenser, but should not allow them to obscure these similarities. We shall need to overcome a sense of incongruity that when it comes to the plunge *in medias res*, Spenser introduces us not to the crisis of some great national event, but to a wandering knight with an ill-assorted retinue—lady, lamb, dwarf—in some undefined wilderness. Of course we do not have long to wait before allegorical meanings begin to show; and we slowly familiarize ourselves, are naturalised in, a unique world, which is Spenser's and no one else's. For we are studying not merely the limited significance of what transpires on the page; we are slowly accumulating the sense of a highly idiosyncratic personality.

That is one of the rewards of the great poem: it is in a high sense personal. Some of the points often made against it disappear in this mature understanding of the work. There is the matter of Spenser's diction, on the whole so lacking in that colloquial vigour which characterizes his contemporary Donne. There is the expansiveness which his invented nine-line stanza does nothing to control. There is, above all, the apparent remoteness of the action from actuality. Yet these objections come to nothing in the end. As for remoteness, Spenser not merely accepted from the theorists of epic the need for it; it was essential to his whole conception. There are passages in the book (like the prophecies of III. iii) which explicitly link these distant events to Tudor England; there are many more in which the reader can act upon hints and do the same. Yet we may get into difficulties when we try to equate a particular figure with a contemporary of Spenser's (Arthegall in the Fifth Book with Lord Grey, for example). And this illustrates what Spenser is about. Certainly he wants us to catch glimpses of Arthegall looking like Lord Grey, or like Essex, or even like Norris; but mostly he shows us a dimly-lit figure in whom we can see persons, or allegories (Arthegall in Book V is also the crocodile, the law without equity) to the degree that we are attuned to his kind of fabling and able to read it. However urgent his meanings, they must be set at this distance; they must be, as it were, a fire for us to read pictures in.

The complaints about diction dissolve in the same way. As Renaissance critics knew, a 'low' or colloquial style would produce in heroic poetry the wrong kind of sharpness and familiarity; and Spenser, who could certainly manage the low style, and could write couplets, saw that even the stanza of Ariosto, though complicated by the additional difficulty of rhyming in English, would not set his themes and narratives at sufficient distance. He made up his new stanza for the same reason that Milton developed his involved syntax: to give to a poetry of 'barbarous' rhyming the magniloquence of an ancient language. As to his deviations from normal usage, they are the verbal parallel of the show and the tournament, which imposed a revived symbolism and a revived chivalry on a modern world, for its own good. They connect the contemporary world with remoter times, set the story at a distance from which its implications are less sharp, more suggestive. Spenser, in short, uses the past, and every kind of distance, so that the reader can grasp something of the possible range of meaning to be found in a poem rooted in his own time. When he chooses he can harden the image, insists on a contemporary application. It is his method to shift and alter focus in this way, with an unexpectedness of transition that reminds one of dreams.

The kind of thing that happens in *The Faerie Queene* can best be explained as the tribute of dream to actuality. A man descends to the underworld, a fleeing maiden divides into two; there are nightmare dualities like Pyrochles and Cymochles, Ollyphant and Argante; Britomart dreams of sexual union with a crocodile; on the way to the Bower, Guyon and the Palmer pass through a seascape Hieronymos Bosch might have conceived; the beautiful Duessa, stripped, is a hideous crone. These are dream figures and transformations; and the dream, with all its shadowy philosophy and sudden immediate relevances, is the dream of a mind haunted by the past, yet actively engaged on the present. The dreamer is a man of subtle imagination and high intelligence, a civilized poet. To deny Spenser high imagination or intelligence, high civility or poetry (and there is a modern habit of doing so) is to forfeit some claim oneself to the possession, even in the humbler degree appropriate to a reader, of these very qualities.

SPENSER'S LIFE

1552 (or 1553 or 1554) Edmund Spenser born in London.

1561 At newly-founded Merchant Taylors School.

1569 Spenser's versions of sonnets by Du Bellay and a *canzone* by Petrarch published in S. John vander Noodt's *Theatre of Voluptuous Worldlings.* (Republished, some in rewritten form, in *Complaints*, 1591.)

    Matriculated at Pembroke Hall, Cambridge, as sizar (poor student). During Cambridge years forms close and lasting friendship with the scholar-critic Gabriel Harvey, Fellow of Pembroke from 1570.

1573 Graduated B.A.

1576 Graduated M.A.

1577 Probably made first visit to Ireland.

1578 Spenser secretary to John Young, bishop of Rochester; then associated with Earl of Leicester, and with his nephew Sidney. Shares with Sidney and Dyer interest in classical reform of English metre.

1579 *The Shepheardes Calender* published, with dedication to Sidney. Probable date of Spenser's first marriage. Spenser wrote all or some of *Mother Hubberds Tale.*

1580 Some of Harvey correspondence published; many projects mentioned, including *The Faerie Queene*, some of which is in Harvey's hands by April. Spenser appointed secretary to Lord Grey de Wilton, new Lord Deputy of Ireland.

1582 Rented New Abbey, outside Dublin. First of conversations with Lodowick Bryskett, including outline of *Faerie Queene*, as recorded in Bryskett's *Discourse of Civill Life*, 1606.

1585 Spenser prebendary of Limerick Cathedral.

1588 Acquired castle of Kilcolman, Co. Cork.

1589 Raleigh visited Spenser at Kilcolman, as recorded in *Colin Clouts Come Home Again.* Raleigh's approval of *Faerie*

    Queene induced Spenser to return with him to London. The
    Queen approved of Spenser's poem.

1590 *The Faerie Queene*, I–III published; dedication to Queen and
    appended Letter to Raleigh. Spenser returned to Ireland.

1591 Spenser published *Complaints*, including *Mother Hubberds Tale*,
    The Ruines of Time, *Muiopotmos*. Also *Daphnaida*, an elegy
    on Lady Douglas Howard, wife of Sir Arthur Gorges.

1592 Publication of translation of the Platonic dialogue *Axiochus*
    by 'Edw. Spenser'.

1594 Married Elizabeth Boyle.

1595 Publication of *Amoretti and Epithalamion*. Publication of *Colin
    Clouts Come Home Again*, with *Astrophel*, the elegy for Sidney.
    Spenser returns to London with *Faerie Queene*, IV–VI.

1596 Publication of *Faerie Queene*, IV–VI and of *Fowre Hymns* and
    Prothalamion, celebrating betrothal of two daughters of
    Earl of Worcester. Spenser returned to Ireland, without the
    reward expected for continuation of *Faerie Queene*.

1598 Appointed Sheriff of Cork. Tyrone's rebellion; sack of Kilcol-
    man. Spenser returned to London, carrying dispatches to
    the Privy Council.

1599 13 January, Spenser died. Buried in Westminster Abbey 'at
    the charges of the Earl of Essex'.

1609 Publication of *Two Cantos of Mutabilitie*.

1633 Publication of *A Vewe of the Present State of Irelande* (written
    about 1596, registered for publication 1598).

SELECT BIBLIOGRAPHY

I. EDITIONS OF SPENSER'S WORKS

The Works of Spenser: a Variorum Edition, ed. Greenlaw, Osgood, Padelford, Heffner and others (Baltimore, 1932–57, 9 vols.).

Poetical Works of Edmund Spenser, ed. J. C. Smith and E. De Sélincourt, (Oxford, 1912).

II. BIOGRAPHY AND CRITICISM

(a) General Studies

H. S. V. Jones, *A Spenser Handbook* (London, 1930: with subsequent editions).

W. L. Renwick, *Edmund Spenser* (London, 1925).

W. Nelson, *The Poetry of Edmund Spenser* (New York, 1963). The best and most modern single-volume study of all the poetry.

(b) Studies of Spenser's Thought

E. Greenlaw, *Studies in Spenser's Historical Allegory* (Baltimore, 1932).

C. S. Lewis, *The Allegory of Love* (Oxford, 1936).

V. K. Whitaker, *The Religious Basis of Spenser's Thought* (Stanford, 1950).

R. Ellrodt, *Neoplatonism in the Poetry of Spenser* (Geneva, 1961).

(c) Studies of The Faerie Queene

J. W. Bennett, *The Evolution of The Faerie Queene* (Chicago, 1942).

A. C. Hamilton, *The Structure of Allegory in The Faerie Queene* (Oxford, 1961).

G. Hough, *A Preface to The Faerie Queene* (London, 1962). Though defective in details, probably the liveliest and most engaging introduction to the poem.

Alastair Fowler, *Spenser and the Numbers of Time* (London, 1964). This reveals complex numerological and astrological patterns in *The Faerie Queene*, and offers striking new interpretations of many passages.

Cs

(*d*) *Studies of the minor poems*:

A. K. Hieatt, *Short Time's Endless Monument* (New York, 1960). A revolutionary book on *Epithalamion*.

P. E. McLane, *Spenser's 'Shepheardes Calender'* (Notre Dame, 1961).

NOTE ON THE TEXT

The text is that of J. C. Smith and E. De Sélincourt in their Oxford edition (1912). The use of *u* and *v* has been normalized. In V. vii. 6, line 9, I have read '*his* wreathed taile' when the 1596 text, accepted by De Sélincourt, has 'her wreathed taile'.

The Shepheardes Calender
(October)

Ægloga decima

ARGUMENT

*In Cuddie is set out the perfecte paterne of a Poete, whiche finding
no maintenaunce of his state and studies, complayneth of the con-
tempte of Poetrie, and the causes thereof: Specially having bene
in all ages, and even amongst the most barbarous alwayes of singu-
lar accounpt and honor, and being indede so worthy and commend-
able an arte: or rather no arte, but a divine gift and heavenly instinct
not to bee gotten by laboure and learning, but adorned with both: and
poured into the witte by a certaine ἐνθουσιασμός. and celestiall
inspiration, as the Author hereof els where at large discourseth,
in his booke called the English Poete, which booke being lately
come to my hands, I mynde also by Gods grace upon further advise-
ment to publish.*

PIERCE   CUDDIE

Cuddie, for shame hold up thy heavye head,
And let us cast with what delight to chace,
And weary thys long lingring *Phœbus* race.
Whilome thou wont the shepheards laddes to leade,
In rymes, in ridles, and in bydding base: 5
Now they in thee, and thou in sleepe art dead.

CUDDIE

Piers, I have pyped erst so long with payne,
That all mine Oten reedes bene rent and wore:
And my poore Muse hath spent her spared store,

Yet little good hath got, and much lesse gayne.   10
Such pleasaunce makes the Grashopper so poore,
And ligge so layd, when Winter doth her straine.

The dapper ditties, that I wont devise,
To feede youthes fancie, and the flocking fry,
Delighten much: what I the bett for thy?   15
They han the pleasure, I a sclender prise.
I beate the bush, the byrds to them doe flye.
What good thereof to Cuddie can arise?

PIRES

Cuddie, the prayse is better, then the price,
The glory eke much greater then the gayne: 20
O what an honor is it, to restraine
The lust of lawlesse youth with good advice:
Or pricke them forth with pleasaunce of thy vaine,
Whereto thou list their trayned willes entice.

Soone as thou gynst to sette thy notes in frame,   25
O how the rurall routes to thee doe cleave:
Seemeth thou dost their soule of sence bereave,
All as the shepheard, that did fetch his dame
From *Plutoes* balefull bowre withouten leave:
His musicks might the hellish hound did tame.   30

CUDDIE

So praysen babes the Peacoks spotted traine,
And wondren at bright *Argus* blazing eye:
But who rewards him ere the more for thy?
Or feedes him once the fuller by a graine?
Sike prayse is smoke, that sheddeth in the skye,   35
Sike words bene wynd, and wasten soone in vayne.

PIERS

Abandon then the base and viler clowne,
Lyft up thy selfe out of the lowly dust:
And sing of bloody Mars, of wars, of giusts,
Turne thee to those, that weld the awful crowne.   40
To doubted Knights, whose woundlesse armour rusts,
And helmes unbruzed wexen dayly browne.

There may thy Muse display her fluttryng wing,
And stretch her selfe at large from East to West:
Whither thou list in fayre *Elisa* rest,   45
Or if thee please in bigger notes to sing,
Advaunce the worthy whome shee loveth best,
That first the white beare to the stake did bring.

And when the stubborne stroke of stronger stounds,
Has somewhat slackt the tenor of thy string: 50
Of love and lustihead tho mayst thou sing,
And carrol lowde, and leade the Myllers rownde,
All were *Elisa* one of thilke same ring.
So mought our *Cuddies* name to Heaven sownde.

CUDDIE

Indeede the Romish *Tityrus*, I heare,   55
Through his *Mecænas* left his Oaten reede,
Whereon he earst had taught his flocks to feede,
And laboured lands to yield the timely eare,
And eft did sing of warres and deadly drede,
So as the Heavens did quake his verse to here.   60

But ah *Mecænas* is yclad in claye,
And great *Augustus* long ygoe is dead:
And all the worthies liggen wrapt in leade,

That matter made for Poets on to play:
For ever, who in derring doe were dreade,   65
The loftie verse of hem was loved aye.

But after vertue gan for age to stoupe,
And mighty manhode brought a bedde of ease.
The vaunting Poets found nought worth a pease,
To put in preace among the learned troupe.   70
Tho gan the streames of flowing wittes to cease,
And sonnebright honour pend in shamefull coupe.

And if that any buddes of Poesie,
Yet of the old stocke gan to shoote agayne:
Or it mens follies mote be forst to fayne,   75
And rolle with rest in rymes of rybaudrye:
Or as it sprong, it wither must agayne:
Tom Piper makes us better melodie.

PIERS

O pierlesse Poesye, where is then thy place?
If nor in Princes pallace thou doe sitt: 80
(And yet is Princes pallace the most fitt)
Ne brest of baser birth doth thee embrace.
Then make thee winges of thine aspyring wit,
And, whence thou camst, flye backe to heaven apace.

CUDDIE

Ah *Percy* it is all to weake and wanne,   85
So high to sore, and make so large a flight:
Her peeced pyneons bene not so in plight,
For *Colin* fittes such famous flight to scanne:
He, were he not with love so ill bedight,
Would mount as high, and sing as soote as Swanne.   90

PIRES

Ah fon, for love does teach him climbe so hie,
And lyftes him up out of the loathsome myre:
Such immortall mirrhor, as he doth admire,
Would rayse ones mynd above the starry skie.
And cause a caytive corage to aspire,   95
For lofty love doth loath a lowly eye.

CUDDIE

All otherwise the state of Poet stands,
For lordly love is such a Tyranne fell:
That where he rules, all power he doth expell.
The vaunted verse a vacant head demaundes,   100
Ne wont with crabbed care the Muses dwell.
Unwisely weaves, that takes two webbes in hand.

Who ever casts to compasse weightye prise,
And thinks to throwe out thondring words of threate:
Let powre in lavish cups and thriftie bitts of meate,   105
For *Bacchus* fruite is frend to *Phœbus* wise.
And when with Wine the braine begins to sweate,
The nombers flowe as fast as spring doth ryse.

Thou kenst not *Percie* howe the ryme should rage.
O if my temples were distain'd with wine,   110
And girt in girlonds of wild Yvie twine,
How I could reare the Muse on stately stage,
And teache her tread aloft in bus-kin fine,
With queint *Bellona* in her equipage.

But ah my corage cooles ere it be warme,   115
For thy, content us in thys humble shade:

Where no such troublous tydes han us assayde,
Here we our slender pipes may safely charme.

PIERS

And when my Gates shall han their bellies layd:
Cuddie shall have a Kidde to store his farme.   120

Cuddies Embleme.
Agitante calescimus illo, &c.

Colin Clouts Come Home Againe
(ll. 835–94)

Of loves perfection perfectly to speake,
Or of his nature rightly to define,
Indeed (said *Colin*) passeth reasons reach,
And needs his priest t'expresse his powre divine.
For long before the world he was y'bore
And bred above in *Venus* bosome deare: 840
For by his powre the world was made of yore,
And all that therein wondrous doth appeare.
For how should else things so far from attone
And so great enemies as of them bee,
Be ever drawne together into one,   845
And taught in such accordance to agree?
Through him the cold began to covet heat,
And water fire; the light to mount on hie,
And th'heauie downe to peize; the hungry t'eat
And voydnesse to seeke full satietie.   850
So being former foes, they wexed friends,

And gan by litle learne to love each other:
So being knit, they brought forth other kynds
Out of the fruitfull wombe of their great mother.
Then first gan heaven out of darknesse dread   855
For to appeare, and brought forth chearfull day:
Next gan the earth to shew her naked head,
Out of deep waters which her drownd alway.
And shortly after, everie living wight
Crept forth like wormes out of her slimie nature,   860
Soone as on them the Suns life giving light,
Had powred kindly heat and formall feature,
Thenceforth they gan each one his like to love,
And like himselfe desire for to beget,
The Lyon chose his mate, the Turtle Dove   865
Her deare, the Dolphin his owne Dolphinet:
But man that had the sparke of reasons might,
More then the rest to rule his passion,
Chose for his love the fairest in his sight.
Like as himselfe was fairest by creation.   870
For beautie is the bayt which with delight
Doth man allure, for to enlarge his kynd,
Beautie the burning lamp of heavens light,
Darting her beames into each feeble mynd:
Against whose powre, nor God nor man can fynd,   875
Defence, ne ward the daunger of the wound,
But being hurt, seeke to be medicynd
Of her that first did stir that mortall stownd.
Then do they cry and call to love apace,
With praiers lowd importuning the skie,   880
Whence he them heares, and when he list shew grace,
Does graunt them grace that otherwise would die.
So love is Lord of all the world by right,
And rules the creatures by his powrfull saw:

All being made the vassalls of his might,   885
Through secret sence which therto doth them draw.
Thus ought all lovers of their lord to deeme:
And with chaste heart to honor him alway:
But who so else doth otherwise esteeme,
Are outlawes, and his lore do disobay.   890
For their desire is base, and doth not merit,
The name of love, but of disloyall lust:
Ne amongst true lovers they shall place inherit,
But as Exuls out of his court be thrust.

Epithalamion

Ye learned sisters which have oftentimes
Beene to me ayding, others to adorne:
Whom ye thought worthy of your gracefull rymes,
That even the greatest did not greatly scorne
To heare theyr names sung in your simple layes,   5
But ioyed in theyr prayse.
And when ye list your owne mishaps to mourne,
Which death, or love, or fortunes wreck did rayse,
Your string could soone to sadder tenor turne,
And teach the woods and waters to lament   10
Your dolefull dreriment.
Now lay those sorrowfull complaints aside,
And having all your heads with girland crownd,
Helpe me mine owne loves prayses to resound,
Ne let the same of any be envide   15
So Orpheus did for his owne bride,
So I unto my selfe alone will sing,
The woods shall to me answer and my Eccho ring.

Early before the worlds light giving lampe,
His golden beame upon the hils doth spred,   20
Having disperst the nights unchearefull dampe,
Doe ye awake, and with fresh lusty hed,
Go to the bowre of my beloved love,
My truest turtle dove,
Bid her awake; for Hymen is awake,   25
And long since ready forth his maske to move,
With his bright Tead that flames with many a flake,
And many a bachelor to waite on him,
In theyr fresh garments trim.
Bid her awake therefore and soone her dight,   30
For lo the wished day is come at last,
That shall for al the paynes and sorrowes past,
Pay to her usury of long delight:
And whylest she doth her dight,
Doe ye to her of ioy and solace sing,   35
That all the woods may answer and your eccho ring.

Bring with you all the Nymphes that you can heare
Both of the rivers and the forrests greene:
And of the sea that neighbours to her neare,
Al with gay girlands goodly wel beseene.   40
And let them also with them bring in hand,
Another gay girland
For my fayre love of lillyes and of roses,
Bound truelove wize with a blew silke riband.
And let them make great store of bridale poses,   45
And let them eeke bring store of other flowers
To deck the bridale bowers.
And let the ground whereas her foot shall tread,
For feare the stones her tender foot should wrong
Be strewed with fragrant flowers all along,   50

And diapred lyke the discolored mead.
Which done, doe at her chamber dore awayt,
For she will waken strayt,
The whiles doe ye this song unto her sing,
The woods shall to you answer and your Eccho ring.   55

Ye Nymphes of Mulla which with carefull heed,
The silver scaly trouts doe tend full well;
And greedy pikes which use therein to feed,
(Those trouts and pikes all others doo excell)
And ye likewise which keepe the rushy lake,   60
Where none doo fishes take,
Bynd up the locks the which hang scatterd light,
And in his waters which your mirror make,
Byhold your faces as the christall bright,
That when you come whereas my love doth lie,   65
No blemish she may spie.
And eke ye lightfoot mayds which keepe the deere,
That on the hoary mountayne use to towre,
And the wylde wolves which seeke them to devoure,
With your steele darts doo chace from comming neer   70
Be also present heere,
To helpe to decke her and to help to sing,
That all the woods may answer and your eccho ring.

Wake, now my love, awake; for it is time,
The Rosy Morne long since left Tithones bed,   75
All ready to her silver coche to clyme,
And Phœbus gins to shew his glorious hed.
Hark how the cheerefull birds do chaunt theyr laies
And carroll of loves praise.
The merry Larke hir mattins sings aloft,   80
The thrush replyes, the Mavis descant playes.

The Ouzell shrills, the Ruddock warbles soft,
So goodly all agree with sweet consent,
To this dayes merriment.
Ah my deere love why doe ye sleepe thus long,   85
When meeter were that ye should now awake,
T'awayt the comming of your ioyous make,
And hearken to the birds lovelearned song,
The deawy leaves among.
For they of ioy and pleasance to you sing,   90
That all the woods them answer and theyr eccho ring.

My love is now awake out of her dreame,
And her fayre eyes like stars that dimmed were
With darksome cloud, now shew theyr goodly beams
More bright then Hesperus his head doth rere.   95
Come now ye damzels, daughters of delight,
Helpe quickly her to dight.
But first come ye fayre houres which were begot
In Ioves sweet paradice, of Day and Night,
Which doe the seasons of the yeare allot,   100
And al that ever in this world is fayre
Doe make and still repayre.
And ye three handmayds of the Cyprian Queene,
The which doe still adorne her beauties pride,
Helpe to addorne my beautifullest bride: 105
And as ye her array, still throw betweene
Some graces to be seene,
And as ye use to Venus, to her sing,
The whiles the woods shal answer and your eccho ring.

Now is my love all ready forth to come,   110
Let all the virgins therefore well awayt,
And ye fresh boyes that tend upon her groome

Prepare your selves; for he is comming strayt.
Set all your things in seemely good aray
Fit for so ioyfull day,   115
The ioyfulst day that ever sunne did see.
Faire Sun, shew forth thy favourable ray,
And let thy lifull heat not fervent be
For feare of burning her sunshyny face,
Her beauty to disgrace.   120
O fayrest Phœbus, father of the Muse,
If ever I did honour thee aright,
Or sing the thing, that mote thy mind delight,
Doe not thy servants simple boone refuse,
But let this day let this one day be myne,   125
Let all the rest be thine.
Then I thy soverayne prayses loud wil sing,
That all the woods shal answer and theyr eccho ring.

Harke how the Minstrels gin to shrill aloud
Their merry Musick that resounds from far,   130
The pipe, the tabor, and the trembling Croud,
That well agree withouten breach or iar.
But most of all the Damzels doe delite,
When they their tymbrels smyte,
And thereunto doe daunce and carrol sweet,   135
That all the sences they doe ravish quite,
The whyles the boyes run up and downe the street,
Crying aloud with strong confused noyce,
As if it were one voyce.
Hymen io Hymen, Hymen they do shout,   140
That even to the heavens theyr shouting shrill
Doth reach, and all the firmament doth fill,
To which the people standing all about,
As in approvance doe thereto applaud

And loud advaunce her laud, 145
And evermore they Hymen Hymen sing,
That al the woods them answer and theyr eccho ring.

Loe where she comes along with portly pace
Lyke Phœbe from her chamber of the East,
Arysing forth to run her mighty race, 150
Clad all in white, that seemes a virgin best.
So well it her beseemes that ye would weene
Some angell she had beene.
Her long loose yellow locks lyke golden wyre,
Sprinckled with perle, and perling flowres a tweene, 155
Doe lyke a golden mantle her attyre,
And being crowned with a girland greene,
Seeme lyke some mayden Queene.
Her modest eyes abashed to behold
So many gazers, as on her do stare, 160
Upon the lowly ground affixed are.
Ne dare lift up her countenance too bold,
But blush to heare her prayses sung so loud,
So farre from being proud.
Nathlesse doe ye still loud her prayses sing. 165
That all the woods may answer and your eccho ring.

Tell me ye merchants daughters did ye see
So fayre a creature in your towne before,
So sweet, so lovely, and so mild as she,
Adornd with beautyes grace and vertues store, 170
Her goodly eyes lyke Saphyres shining bright,
Her forehead yvory white,
Her cheekes lyke apples which the sun hath rudded,
Her lips lyke cherryes charming men to byte,
Her brest like to a bowle of creame uncrudded, 175

Ds

Her paps lyke lyllies budded,
Her snowie necke lyke to a marble towre,
And all her body like a pallace fayre,
Ascending uppe with many a stately stayre,
To honors seat and chastities sweet bowre.   180
Why stand ye still ye virgins in amaze,
Upon her so to gaze,
Whiles ye forget your former lay to sing,
To which the woods did answer and your eccho ring.

But if ye saw that which no eyes can see,   185
The inward beauty of her lively spright,
Garnisht with heavenly guifts of high degree,
Much more then would ye wonder at that sight,
And stand astonisht lyke to those which red
Medusaes mazeful hed.   190
There dwels sweet love and constant chastity,
Unspotted fayth and comely womanhood,
Regard of honour and mild modesty,
There vertue raynes as Queen in royal throne,
And giveth lawes alone.   195
The which the base affections doe obay,
And yeeld theyr services unto her will,
Ne thought of thing uncomely ever may
Thereto approch to tempt her mind to ill.
Had ye once seene these her celestial threasures,   200
And unrevealed pleasures,
Then would ye wonder and her prayses sing,
That al the woods should answer and your echo ring.

Open the temple gates unto my love,
Open them wide that she may enter in,   205
And all the postes adorne as doth behove,

And all the pillours deck with girlands trim,
For to recyve this Saynt with honour dew,
That commeth in to you.
With trembling steps and humble reverence,   210
She commeth in, before th'almighties vew,
Of her ye virgins learne obedience,
When so ye come into those holy places,
To humble your proud faces:
Bring her up to th'high altar, that she may   215
The sacred ceremonies there partake,
The which do endlesse matrimony make,
And let the roring Organs loudly play
The praises of the Lord in lively notes,
The whiles with hollow throates   220
The Choristers the ioyous Antheme sing,
That al the woods may answere and their eccho ring.

Behold whiles she before the altar stands
Hearing the holy priest that to her speakes
And blesseth her with his two happy hands,   225
How the red roses flush up in her cheekes,
And the pure snow with goodly vermill stayne,
Like crimsin dyde in grayne,
That even th'Angels which continually,
About the sacred Altare doe remaine,   230
Forget their service and about her fly;
Ofte peeping in her face that seemes more fayre,
The more they on it stare.
But her sad eyes still fastened on the ground,
Are governed with goodly modesty,   235
That suffers not one looke to glaunce awry,
Which may let in a little thought unsownd.
Why blush ye love to give to me your hand,

The pledge of all our band?
Sing ye sweet Angels, Alleluya sing,   240
That all the woods may answere and your eccho ring.

Now al is done; bring home the bride againe,
Bring home the triumph of our victory,
Bring home with you the glory of her gaine,
With ioyance bring her and with iollity.   245
Never had man more ioyfull day then this,
Whom heaven would heape with blis.
Make feast therefore now all this live long day,
This day for ever to me holy is,
Poure out the wine without restraint or stay,   250
Poure not by cups, but by the belly full,
Poure out to all that wull,
And sprinkle all the postes and wals with wine,
That they may sweat, and drunken be withall.
Crowne ye God Bacchus with a coronall,   255
And Hymen also crowne with wreathes of vine,
And let the Graces daunce unto the rest;
For they can doo it best:
The whiles the maydens doe theyr carroll sing,
To which the woods shal answer and theyr eccho ring.   260

Ring ye the bels, ye yong men of the towne,
And leave your wonted labors for this day:
This day is holy; doe ye write it downe,
That ye for ever it remember may.
This day the sunne is in his chiefest hight,   265
With Barnaby the bright,
From whence declining daily by degrees,
He somewhat loseth of his heat and light,
When once the Crab behind his back he sees.

But for this time it ill ordained was,   270
To chose the longest day in all the yeare,
And shortest night, when longest fitter weare:
Yet never day so long, but late would passe.
Ring ye the bels, to make it weare away,
And bonefiers make all day,   275
And daunce about them, and about them sing
That all the woods may answer, and your eccho ring.

Ah when will this long weary day have end,
And lende me leave to come unto my love?
How slowly do the houres theyr numbers spend?   280
How slowly does sad Time his feathers move?
Hast thee O fayrest Planet to thy home
Within the Westerne fome:
Thy tyred steedes long since have need of rest.
Long though it be, at last I see it gloome,   285
And the bright evening star with golden creast
Appeare out of the East.
Fayre childe of beauty, glorious lampe of love
That all the host of heaven in rankes doost lead,
And guydest lovers through the nightes dread,   290
How chearefully thou lookest from above,
And seemst to laugh atweene thy twinkling light
As ioying in the sight
Of these glad many which for ioy doe sing,
That all the woods them answer and their eccho ring.   295

Now ceasse ye damsels your delights forepast;
Enough is it, that all the day was youres:
Now day is doen, and night is nighing fast:
Now bring the Bryde into the brydall boures.

Now night is come, now soone her disaray, 300
And in her bed her lay;
Lay her in lillies and in violets,
And silken courteins over her display,
And odourd sheetes, and Arras coverlets.
Behold how goodly my faire love does ly 305
In proud humility;
Like unto Maia, when as Iove her tooke,
In Tempe, lying on the flowry gras,
Twixt sleepe and wake, after she weary was,
With bathing in the Acidalian brooke. 310
Now it is night, ye damsels may be gon,
And leave my love alone,
And leave likewise your former lay to sing:
The woods no more shal answere, nor your eccho ring.

Now welcome night, thou night so long expected, 315
That long daies labour doest at last defray,
And all my cares, which cruell love collected,
Hast sumd in one, and cancelled for aye:
Spread thy broad wing over my love and me,
That no man may us see, 320
And in thy sable mantle us enwrap,
From feare of perrill and foule horror free.
Let no false treason seeke us to entrap,
Nor any dread disquiet once annoy
The safety of our ioy: 325
But let the night be calme and quietsome,
Without tempestuous storms or sad afray:
Lyke as when Iove with fayre Alcmena lay,
When he begot the great Tirynthian groome:
Or lyke as when he with thy selfe did lie, 330
And begot Maiesty.

And let the mayds and yongmen cease to sing:
Ne let the woods them answer, nor theyr eccho ring.

Let no lamenting cryes, nor dolefull teares,
Be heard all night within nor yet without: 335
Ne let false whispers, breeding hidden feares,
Breake gentle sleepe with misconceived dout.
Let no deluding dreames, nor dreadful sights
Make sudden sad affrights;
Ne let housefyres, nor lightnings helpelesse harmes, 340
Ne let the Pouke, nor other evill sprights,
Ne let mischivous witches with theyr charmes,
Ne let hob Goblins, names whose sence we see not,
Fray us with things that be not,
Let not the shriech Oule, nor the Storke be heard: 345
Nor the night Raven that still deadly yels,
Nor damned ghosts cald up with mighty spels,
Nor griesly vultures make us once affeard:
Ne let th'unpleasant Quyre of Frogs still croking
Make us to wish theyr choking. 350
Let none of these theyr drery accents sing;
Ne let the woods them answer, nor theyr eccho ring.

But let stil Silence trew night watches keepe,
That sacred peace may in assurance rayne,
And tymely sleep, when it is tyme to sleepe, 355
May poure his limbs forth on your pleasant playne,
The whiles an hundred little winged loves,
Like divers fethered doves,
Shall fly and flutter round about your bed,
And in the secret darke, that none reproves, 360
Their prety stealthes shal worke, and snares shal spread

To filch away sweet snatches of delight,
Conceald through covert night.
Ye sonnes of Venus, play your sports at will,
For greedy pleasure, carelesse of your toyes, 365
Thinks more upon her paradise of ioyes,
Then what ye do, albe it good or ill.
All night therefore attend your merry play,
For it will soone be day:
Now none doth hinder you, that say or sing, 370
Ne will the woods now answer, nor your Eccho ring.

Who is the same, which at my window peepes?
Or whose is that faire face, that shines so bright,
Is it not Cinthia, she that never sleepes,
But walkes about high heaven al the night? 375
O fayrest goddesse, do thou not envy
My love with me to spy:
For thou likewise didst love, though now unthought,
And for a fleece of woll, which privily,
The Latmian shephard once unto thee brought, 380
His pleasures with thee wrought.
Therefore to us be favorable now;
And sith of wemens labours thou hast charge,
And generation goodly dost enlarge,
Encline thy will t'effect our wishfull vow, 385
And the chast wombe informe with timely seed,
That may our comfort breed:
Till which we cease our hopefull hap to sing,
Ne let the woods us answere, nor our Eccho ring.

And thou great Iuno, which with awful might 390
The lawes of wedlock still dost patronize,

And the religion of the faith first plight
With sacred rites hast taught to solemnize:
And eeke for comfort often called art
Of women in their smart,   395
Eternally bind thou this lovely band,
And all thy blessings unto us impart.
And thou glad Genius, in whose gentle hand,
The bridale bowre and geniall bed remaine,
Without blemish or staine,   400
And the sweet pleasures of theyr loves delight
With secret ayde doest succour and supply,
Till they bring forth the fruitfull progeny,
Send us the timely fruit of this same night.
And thou fayre Hebe, and thou Hymen free,   405
Grant that it may so be.
Til which we cease your further prayse to sing,
Ne any woods shal answer, nor your Eccho ring.

And ye high heavens, the temple of the gods,
In which a thousand torches flaming bright   410
Doe burne, that to us wretched earthly clods,
In dreadful darknesse lend desired light;
And all ye powers which in the same remayne,
More then we men can fayne,
Poure out your blessing on us plentiously,   415
And happy influence upon us raine,
That we may raise a large posterity,
Which from the earth, which they may long possesse,
With lasting happinesse,
Up to your haughty pallaces may mount,   420
And for the guerdon of theyr glorious merit
May heavenly tabernacles there inherit,
Of blessed Saints for to increase the count.

So let us rest, sweet love, in hope of this,
And cease till then our tymely ioyes to sing,   425
The woods no more us answer, nor our eccho ring.

Song made in lieu of many ornaments,
With which my love should duly have bene dect,
Which cutting off through hasty accidents,
Ye would not stay your dew time to expect,   430
But promist both to recompens,
Be unto her a goodly ornament,
And for short time an endlesse moniment.

The Faerie Queene

A Letter of the Authors expounding his
whole intention in the course of this worke: which
for that it giveth great light to the Reader, for
the better understanding is hereunto annexed

To the Right noble, and Valorous, Sir Walter Raleigh knight,
Lo. Wardein of the Stanneryes, and her Maiesties liefe-
tenaunt of the County of Cornewayll.

Sir knowing how doubtfully all Allegories may be construed,
and this booke of mine, which I have entituled the Faery Queene,
being a continued Allegory, or darke conceit, I have thought
good aswell for avoyding of gealous opinions and misconstruc-
tions, as also for your better light in reading thereof, (being so   5
by you commanded,) to discover unto you the general intention
and meaning, which in the whole course thereof I have fashioned,
without expressing of any particular purposes or by-accidents
therein occasioned. The generall end therefore of all the booke

is to fashion a gentleman or noble person in vertuous and gentle 10
discipline: Which for that I conceived shoulde be most plausible
and pleasing, being coloured with an historicall fiction, the which
the most part of men delight to read, rather for variety of matter,
then for profite of the ensample: I chose the historye of king
Arthure, as most fitte for the excellency of his person, being made 15
famous by many mens former workes, and also furthest from
the daunger of envy, and suspition of present time. In which
I have followed all the antique Poets historicall, first Homere,
who in the Persons of Agamemnon and Ulysses hath ensampled
a good governour and a vertuous man, the one in his Ilias, the 20
other in his Odysseis: then Virgil, whose like intention was to
doe in the person of Aeneas: after him Ariosto comprised them
both in his Orlando: and lately Tasso dissevered them againe,
and formed both parts in two persons, namely that part which
they in Philosophy call Ethice, or vertues of a private man, 25
coloured in his Rinaldo: The other named Politice in his God-
fredo. By ensample of which excellente Poets, I labour to
pourtraict in Arthure, before he was king, the image of a brave
knight, perfected in the twelve private morall vertues, as Aristotle
hath devised, the which is the purpose of these first twelve 30
bookes: which if I finde to be well accepted, I may be perhaps
encoraged, to frame the other part of polliticke vertues in his
person, after that hee came to be king. To some I know this
Methode will seeme displeasaunt, which had rather have good
discipline delivered plainly in way of precepts, or sermoned at 35
large, as they use, then thus clowdily enwrapped in Allegoricall
devises. But such, me seeme, should be satisfide with the use of
these dayes, seeing all things accounted by their showes, and
nothing esteemed of, that is not delightfull and pleasing to com-
mune sence. For this cause is Xenophon preferred before Plato, 40
for that the one in the exquisite depth of his iudgement, formed
a Commune welth such as it should be, but the other in the

person of *Cyrus* and the *Persians* fashioned a governement such as might best be: So much more profitable and gratious is doctrine by ensample, then by rule. So have I laboured to doe 45 in the person of *Arthure*: whome I conceive after his long education by *Timon*, to whom he was by *Merlin* delivered to be brought up, so soone as he was borne of the Lady *Igrayne*, to have seene in a dream or vision the *Faery Queen*, with whose excellent beauty ravished, he awaking resolved to seeke her out, 50 and so being by *Merlin* armed, and by *Timon* throughly instructed, he went to seeke her forth in *Faerye* land. In that *Faery Queene* I meane glory in my generall intention, but in my particular I conceive the most excellent and glorious person of our soveraine the *Queene*, and her kingdome in *Faery* land. And 55 yet in some places els, I doe otherwise shadow her. For considering she beareth two persons, the one of a most royall *Queene* or *Empresse*, the other of a most vertuous and beautifull *Lady*, this latter part in some places I doe expresse in *Belphœbe*, fashioning her name according to your owne excellent con- 60 ceipt of *Cynthia*, (*Phœbe* and *Cynthia* being both names of *Diana*.) So in the person of Prince *Arthure* I sette forth magnificence in particular, which vertue for that (according to *Aristotle* and the rest) it is the perfection of all the rest, and conteineth in it them all, therefore in the whole course I 65 mention the deedes of *Arthure* applyable to that vertue, which I write of in that booke. But of the xii. other vertues, I make xii. other knights the patrones, for the more variety of the history: Of which these three bookes contayn three, The first of the knight of the *Redcrosse*, in whome I expresse Holynes: The 70 seconde of Sir *Guyon*, in whome I sette forth Temperaunce: The third of *Britomartis* a Lady knight, in whome I picture Chastity. But because the beginning of the whole worke seemeth abrupte and as depending upon other antecedents, it needs that ye know the occasion of these three knights severall adventures. For 75

the *Methode of a Poet historical is not such, as of an Historiographer. For an Historiographer discourseth of affayres orderly
as they were donne, accounting as well the times as the actions,
but a Poet thrusteth into the middest, even where it most con-
cerneth him, and there recoursing to the thinges forepaste, and 80
divining of thinges to come, maketh a pleasing Analysis of all.
The beginning therefore of my history, if it were to be told by an
Historiographer, should be the twelfth booke, which is the
last, where I devise that the Faery Queene kept her Annuall
feaste xii. dayes, uppon which xii. severall dayes, the occasions 85
of the xii. severall adventures hapned, which being undertaken
by xii. severall knights, are in these xii books severally handled
and discoursed. The first was this. In the beginning of the feast,
there presented him selfe a tall clownishe younge man, who
falling before the Queen of Faries desired a boone (as the manner 90
then was) which during that feast she might not refuse: which
was that hee might have the atchievement of any adventure,
which during that feaste should happen, that being graunted,
he rested him on the floore, unfitte through his rusticity for a
better place. Soone after entred a faire Ladye in mourning 95
weedes, riding on a white Asse, with a dwarfe behind her
leading a warlike steed, that bore the Armes of a knight, and
his speare in the dwarfes hand. Shee falling before the Queene
of Faeries, complayned that her father and mother an ancient
King and Queene, had bene by an huge dragon many years 100
shut up in a brasen Castle, who thence suffred them not to
yssew: and therefore besought the Faery Queene to assygne her
some one of her knights to take on him that exployt. Presently
that clownish person upstarting, desired that adventure:
whereat the Queene much wondering, and the Lady much 105
gainesaying yet he earnestly importuned his desire. In the
end the Lady told him that unlesse that armour which she
brought, would serve him (that is the armour of a Christian*

man specified by Saint Paul v. Ephes.) that he could not
succeed in that enterprise, which being forthwith put upon 110
him with dewe furnitures thereunto, he seemed the goodliest
man in al that company, and was well liked of the Lady. And
eftesoones taking on him knighthood, and mounting on that
straunge Courser, he went forth with her on that adventure:
where beginneth the first booke, vz.   115

A gentle knight was pricking on the playne, &c.

The second day ther came in a Palmer bearing an Infant
with bloody hands, whose Parents he complained to have bene
slayn by an Enchaunteresse called Acrasia: and therfore craved
of the Faery Queene, to appoint him some knight, to performe 120
that adventure, which being assigned to Sir Guyon, he presently
went forth with that same Palmer: which is the beginning of
the second booke and the whole subiect thereof. The third
day there came in, a Groome who complained before the
Faery Queene, that a vile Enchaunter called Busirane had in 125
hand a most faire Lady called Amoretta, whom he kept in most
grievous torment, because she would not yield him the pleasure
of her body. Whereupon Sir Scudamour the lover of that Lady
presently tooke on him that adventure. But being unable to performe it by reason of the hard Enchauntments, after long 130
sorrow, in the end met with Britomartis, who succoured him,
and reskewed his love.

But by occasion hereof, many other adventures are intermedled, but rather as Accidents, then intendments. As the love
of Britomart, the overthrow of Marinell, the misery of 135
Florimell, the vertuousnes of Belphœbe, the lasciviousnes of
Hellenora, and many the like.

Thus much Sir, I have briefly overronne to direct your
understanding to the wel-head of the History, that from thence
gathering the whole intention of the conceit, ye may as in a 140

*handfull gripe al the discourse, which otherwise may happily
seeme tedious and confused. So humbly craving the continuaunce
of your honorable favour towards me, and th'eternall establishment of your happines, I humbly take leave.*

23. Ianuary. 1589 145

Yours most humbly affectionate.

Ed. Spenser.

The Faerie Queene. Book I

Canto i, 1–27

1

A Gentle Knight was pricking on the plaine,
  Y cladd in mightie armes and silver shielde,
  Wherein old dints of deepe wounds did remaine,
  The cruell markes of many' a bloudy fielde;
  Yet armes till that time did he never wield: 5
  His angry steede did chide his foming bitt,
  As much disdayning to the curbe to yield:
  Full iolly knight he seemd, and faire did sitt,
As one for knightly giusts and fierce encounters fitt.

2

But on his brest a bloudie Crosse he bore,   10
  The deare remembrance of his dying Lord,
  For whose sweete sake that glorious badge he wore,
  And dead as living ever him ador'd:
  Upon his shield the like was also scor'd,
  For soveraine hope, which in his helpe he had: 15

Right faithfull true he was in deede and word,
  But of his cheere did seeme too solemne sad;
Yet nothing did he dread, but ever was ydrad.

3

Upon a great adventure he was bond,
  That greatest *Gloriana* to him gave,   20
  That greatest Glorious Queene of *Faerie* lond,
  To winne him worship, and her grace to have,
  Which of all earthly things he most did crave;
  And ever as he rode, his hart did earne
  To prove his puissance in battell brave   25
  Upon his foe, and his new force to learne;
Upon his foe, a Dragon horrible and stearne.

4

A lovely Ladie rode him faire beside,
  Upon a lowly Asse more white then snow,
  Yet she much whiter, but the same did hide   30
  Under a vele, that wimpled was full low,
  And over all a blacke stole she did throw,
  As one that inly mournd: so was she sad,
  And heavie sat upon her palfrey slow:
  Seemed in heart some hidden care she had,   35
And by her in a line a milke white lambe she lad.

5

So pure an innocent, as that same lambe,
  She was in life and every vertuous lore,
  And by descent from Royall lynage came
  Of ancient Kings and Queenes, that had of yore   40
  Their scepters stretcht from East to Westerne shore,

And all the world in their subiection held;
Till that infernall feend with foule uprore
Forwasted all their land, and them expeld:
Whom to avenge, she had this Knight from far compeld. 45

6

Behind her farre away a Dwarfe did lag,
  That lasie seemd in being ever last,
  Or wearied with bearing of her bag
  Of needments at his backe.   Thus as they past,
  The day with cloudes was suddeine overcast,   50
  And angry *Iove* an hideous storme of raine
  Did poure into his Lemans lap so fast,
  That every wight to shrowd it did constrain,
And this faire couple eke to shroud themselves were fain.

7

Enforst to seeke some covert nigh at hand,   55
  A shadie grove not far away they spide,
  That promist ayde the tempest to withstand:
  Whose loftie trees yclad with sommers pride,
  Did spred so broad, that heavens light did hide,
  Not perceable with power of any starre: 60
  And all within were pathes and alleies wide,
  With footing worne, and leading inward farre:
Faire harbour that them seemes; so in they entred arre.

8

And foorth they passe, with pleasure forward led,
  Ioying to heare the birdes sweete harmony,   65
  Which therein shrouded from the tempest dred,
  Seemd in their song to scorne the cruell sky.
  Much can they prayse the trees so straight and hy,

   E5

The sayling Pine, the Cedar proud and tall,
The vine-prop Elme, the Poplar never dry,   70
The builder Oake, sole king of forrests all,
The Aspine good for staves, the Cypresse funerall.

9

The Laurell, meed of mightie Conquerours
  And Poets sage, the Firre that weepeth still,
  The Willow worne of forlorne Paramours,   75
  The Eugh obedient to the benders will,
  The Birch for shaftes, the Sallow for the mill,
  The Mirrhe sweete bleeding in the bitter wound,
  The warlike Beech, the Ash for nothing ill,
  The fruitfull Olive, and the Platane round,   80
The carver Holme, the Maple seeldom inward sound.

10

Led with delight, they thus beguile the way,
  Untill the blustring storme is overblowne;
  When weening to returne, whence they did stray,
  They cannot finde that path, which first was showne,   85
  But wander too and fro in wayes unknowne,
  Furthest from end then, when they neerest weene,
  That makes them doubt, their wits be not their owne:
  So many pathes, so many turnings seene,
That which of them to take, in diverse doubt they been.   90

11

At last resolving forward still to fare,
  Till that some end they finde or in or out,
  That path they take, that beaten seemd most bare
  And like to lead the labyrinth about;
  Which when by tract they hunted had throughout,   95

At length it brought them to a hollow cave,
  Amid the thickest woods.   The Champion stout
Eftsoones dismounted from his courser brave,
And to the Dwarfe a while his needlesse spere he gave.

12

Be well aware, quoth then that Ladie milde,   100
  Least suddaine mischiefe ye too rash provoke:
  The danger hid, the place unknowne and wilde,
  Breedes dreadfull doubts: Oft fire is without smoke,
  And perill without show: therefore your stroke
  Sir knight with-hold, till further triall made.   105
  Ah Ladie (said he) shame were to revoke
  The forward footing for an hidden shade:
Vertue gives her selfe light, through darkenesse for to
    wade.

13

Yea but (quoth she) the perill of this place
  I better wot then you, though now too late   110
  To wish you backe returne with foule disgrace,
  Yet wisedome warnes, whilest foot is in the gate,
  To stay the steppe, ere forced to retrate.
  This is the wandring wood, this *Errours den*,
  A monster vile, whom God and man does hate: 115
  Therefore I read beware.   Fly fly (quoth then
The fearefull Dwarfe:) this is no place for living men.

14

But full of fire and greedy hardiment,
  The youthfull knight could not for ought be staide,
  But forth unto the darksome hole he went,   120
  And looked in: his glistring armor made

A litle glooming light, much like a shade,
By which he saw the ugly monster plaine,
Halfe like a serpent horribly displaide,
But th'other halfe did womans shape retaine,   125
Most lothsom, filthie, foule, and full of vile disdaine.

15

And as she lay upon the durtie ground,
Her huge long taile her den all overspred,
Yet was in knots and many boughtes upwound,
Pointed with mortall sing.   Of her there bred   130
A thousand yong ones, which she dayly fed,
Sucking upon her poisonous dugs, eachone
Of sundry shapes, yet all ill favored:
Soone as that uncouth light upon them shone,
Into her mouth they crept, and suddain all were gone.   135

16

Their dam upstart, out of her den effraide,
And rushed forth, hurling her hideous taile
About her cursed head, whose folds displaid
Were stretcht now forth at length without entraile.
She lookt about, and seeing one in mayle   140
Armed to point, sought backe to turne againe;
For light she hated as the deadly bale,
Ay wont in desert darknesse to remaine,
Where plaine none might her see, nor she see any plaine.

17

Which when the valiant Elfe perceiv'd, he lept   145
As Lyon fierce upon the flying pray,
And with his trenchand blade her boldly kept
From turning backe, and forced her to stay:

Therewith enrag'd she loudly gan to bray,
  And turning fierce, her speckled taile advaunst,   150
  Threatning her angry sting, him to dismay:
  Who nought aghast, his mightie hand enhaunst:
The stroke down from her head unto her shoulder glaunst.

18

Much daunted with that dint, her sence was dazd,
  Yet kindling rage, her selfe she gathered round,   155
  And all attonce her beastly body raizd
  With doubled forces high above the ground:
  Tho wrapping up her wrethed sterne arownd,
  Lept fierce upon his shield, and her huge traine
  All suddenly about his body wound,   160
  That hand or foot to stirre he strove in vaine:
God helpe the man so wrapt in *Errours* endlesse traine.

19

His Lady sad to see his sore constraint,
  Cride out, Now now Sir knight, shew what ye bee,
  Add faith unto your force, and be not faint: 165
  Strangle her, else she sure will strangle thee.
  That when he heard, in great perplexitie,
  His gall did grate for griefe and high disdaine,
  And knitting all his force got one hand free,
  Wherewith he grypt her gorge with so great paine,   170
That soone to loose her wicked bands did her constraine.

20

Therewith she spewd out of her filthy maw
  A floud of poyson horrible and blacke,
  Full of great lumpes of flesh and gobbets raw,
  Which stunck so vildly, that it forst him slacke   175

His grasping hold, and from her turne him backe:
  Her vomit full of bookes and papers was,
  With loathly frogs and toades, which eyes did lacke,
  And creeping sought way in the weedy gras:
Her filthy parbreake all the place defiled has.   180

21

As when old father *Nilus* gins to swell
  With timely pride above the *Aegyptian* vale.
  His fattie waves do fertile slime outwell,
  And overflow each plaine and lowly dale:
  But when his later spring gins to avale,   185
  Huge heapes of mudd he leaves, wherein there breed
  Ten thousand kindes of creatures, partly male
  And partly female of his fruitfull seed;
Such ugly monstrous shapes elswhere may no man reed.

22

The same so sore annoyed has the knight,   190
  That welnigh choked with the deadly stinke,
  His forces faile, ne can no longer fight.
  Whose corage when the feend perceiv'd to shrinke,
  She poured forth out of her hellish sinke
  Her fruitfull cursed spawne of serpents small,   195
  Deformed monsters, fowle, and blacke as inke,
  Which swarming all about his legs did crall,
And him encombred sore, but could not hurt at all.

23

As gentle Shepheard in sweete even-tide,
  When ruddy *Phœbus* gins to welke in west,   200
  High on an hill, his flocke to vewen wide,
  Markes which do byte their hasty supper best;

A cloud of combrous gnattes do him molest,
All striving to infixe their feeble stings,
That from their noyance he no where can rest,   205
But with his clownish hands their tender wings
He brusheth oft, and oft doth mar their murmurings,

24

Thus ill bestedd, and fearefull more of shame,
Then of the certaine perill he stood in,
Halfe furious unto his foe he came,   210
Resolv'd in minde all suddenly to win,
Or soone to lose, before he once would lin;
And strooke at her with more then manly force,
That from her body full of filthie sin
He raft her hatefull head without remorse;   215
A streame of cole black bloud forth gushed from her
    corse.

25

Her scattred brood, soone as their Parent deare
They saw so rudely falling to the ground,
Groning full deadly, all with troublous feare,
Gathred themselves about her body round,   220
Weening their wonted entrance to have found
At her wide mouth: but being there withstood
They flocked all about her bleeding wound,
And sucked up their dying mothers blood,
Making her death their life, and eke her hurt their good.   225

26

That detestable sight him much amazde,
To see th'unkindly Impes of heaven accurst,
Devoure their dam; on whom while so he gazd,

Having all satisfide their bloudy thurst,
Their bellies swolne he saw with fulnesse burst,   230
And bowels gushing forth: well worthy end
Of such as drunke her life, the which them nurst;
Now needeth him no lenger labour spend,
His foes have slaine themselves, with whom he should
    contend.

27

His Ladie seeing all, that chaunst, from farre   235
    Approcht in hast to greet his victorie,
    And said, Faire knight, borne under happy starre,
    Who see your vanquisht foes before you lye;
    Well worthy be you of that Armorie,
    Wherein ye have great glory wonne this day,   240
    And proov'd your strength on a strong enimie,
    Your first adventure: many such I pray,
And henceforth ever wish, that like succeed it may.

I. ii, 20–26

20

The Lady when she saw her champion fall,
    Like the old ruines of a broken towre,   245
    Staid not to waile his woefull funerall,
    But from him fled away with all her powre;
    Who after her as hastily gan scowre,
    Bidding the Dwarfe with him to bring away
    The *Sarazins* shield, signe of the conqueroure.   250
    Her soone he overtooke, and bad to stay,
For present cause was none of dread her to dismay.

21

She turning backe with ruefull countenaunce,
  Cride, Mercy mercy Sir vouchsafe to show
  On silly Dame, subiect to hard mischaunce,   255
  And to your mighty will. Her humblesse low
  In so ritch weedes and seeming glorious show,
  Did much emmove his stout heroicke heart,
  And said, Deare dame, your suddein over-throw
  Much rueth me; but now put feare apart,   260
And tell, both who ye be, and who that tooke your part.

22

Melting in teares, then gan she thus lament;
  The wretched woman, whom unhappy howre
  Hath now made thrall to your commandement,
  Before that angry heavens list to lowre,   265
  And fortune false betraide me to your powre
  Was, (O what now availeth that I was!)
  Borne the sole daughter of an Emperour,
  He that the wide West under his rule has,
And high hath set his throne, where *Tiberis* doth pas.   270

23

He in the first flowre of my freshest age,
  Betrothed me unto the onely haire
  Of a most mighty king, most rich and sage;
  Was never Prince so faithfull and so faire,
  Was never Prince so meeke and debonaire;   275
  But ere my hoped day of spousall shone,
  My dearest Lord fell from high honours staire,
  Into the hands of his accursed fone,
And cruelly was slaine, that shall I ever mone.

24

His blessed body spoild of lively breath,   280
  Was afterward, I know not how, convaid
  And fro me hid: of whose most innocent death
  When tidings came to me unhappy maid,
  O how great sorrow my sad soule assaid.
  Then forth I went his woefull corse to find,   285
  And many yeares throughout the world I straid,
  A virgin widow, whose deepe wounded mind
With love, long time did languish as the striken hind.

25

At last it chaunced this proud *Sarazin*
  To meete me wandring, who perforce me led   290
  With him away, but yet could never win
  The Fort, that Ladies hold in soveraigne dread.
  There lies he now with foule dishonour dead,
  Who whiles he liv'de, was called proud *Sans foy*,
  The eldest of three brethren, all three bred   295
  Of one bad sire, whose youngest is *Sans ioy*,
And twixt them both was borne the bloudy bold *Sans loy*.

26

In this sad plight, friendlesse, unfortunate,
  Now miserable I *Fidessa* dwell,
  Craving of you in pitty of my state,   300
  To do none ill, if please ye not do well.
  He in great passion all this while did dwell,
  More busying his quicke eyes, her face to view,
  Then his dull eares, to heare what she did tell;
  And said, Faire Lady hart of flint would rew   305
The undeserved woes and sorrowes, which ye shew.

I. iv. 17-37

17

So forth she comes, and to her coche does clyme,
   Adorned all with gold, and girlonds gay,
   That seemd as fresh as *Flora* in her prime,
   And strove to match, in royall rich array,   310
   Great *Iunoes* golden chaire, the which they say
   The Gods stand gazing on, when she does ride
   To *Ioves* high house through heavens braspaved way
   Drawne of faire Pecocks, that excell in pride,
And full of *Argus* eyes their tailes dispredden wide.   315

18

But this was drawne of six unequall beasts,
   On which her six sage Counsellours did ryde,
   Taught to obay their bestiall beheasts,
   With like conditions to their kinds applyde:
   Of which the first, that all the rest did guyde,   320
   Was sluggish *Idlenesse* the nourse of sin;
   Upon a slouthfull Asse he chose to ryde,
   Arayd in habit blacke, and amis thin,
Like to an holy Monck, the service to begin.

19

And in his hand his Portesse still he bare,   325
   That much was worne, but therein little red,
   For of devotion he had little care,
   Still drownd in sleepe, and most of his dayes ded;
   Scarse could he once uphold his heavie hed,
   To looken, whether it were night or day: 330
   May seeme the wayne was very evill led,
   When such an one had guiding of the way,
That knew not, whether right he went, or else astray.

20

From worldly cares himselfe he did esloyne,
  And greatly shunned manly exercise,   335
  From every worke he chalenged essoyne,
  For contemplation sake: yet otherwise,
  His life he led in lawlesse riotise;
  By which he grew to grievous malady;
  For in his lustlesse limbs through evill guise   340
  A shaking fever raignd continually:
Such one was *Idlenesse*, first of this company.

21

And by his side rode loathsome *Gluttony*,
  Deformed creature, on a filthie swyne,
  His belly was up-blowne with luxury,   345
  And eke with fatnesse swollen were his eyne,
  And like a Crane his necke was long and fyne,
  With which he swallowd up excessive feast,
  For want whereof poore people oft did pyne;
  And all the way, most like a brutish beast,   350
He spued up his gorge, that all did him deteast.

22

In greene vine leaves he was right fitly clad;
  For other clothes he could not weare for heat,
  And on his head an yvie girland had,
  From under which fast trickled downe the sweat: 355
  Still as he rode, he somewhat still did eat,
  And in his hand did beare a bouzing can,
  Of which he supt so oft, that on his seat
  His dronken corse he scarse upholden can,
In shape and life more like a monster, then a man.   360

23

Unfit he was for any worldly thing,
  And eke unhable once to stirre or go,
  Not meet to be of counsell to a king,
  Whose mind in meat and drinke was drowned so,
  That from his friend he seldome knew his fo: 365
  Full of diseases was his carcas blew,
  And a dry dropsie through his flesh did flow:
  Which by misdiet daily greater grew:
Such one was *Gluttony*, the second of that crew.

24

And next to him rode lustfull *Lechery*,   370
  Upon a bearded Goat, whose rugged haire,
  And whally eyes (the signe of gelosy,)
  Was like the person selfe, whom he did beare:
  Who rough, and blacke, and filthy did appeare,
  Unseemely man to please faire Ladies eye;   375
  Yet he of Ladies oft was loved deare,
  When fairer faces were bid standen by:
O who does know the bent of womens fantasy?

25

In a greene gowne he clothed was full faire,
  Which underneath did hide his filthinesse,   380
  And in his hand a burning hart he bare,
  Full of vaine follies, and new fanglenesse:
  For he was false, and fraught with ficklenesse,
  And learned had to love with secret lookes,
  And well could daunce, and sing with ruefulnesse,   385
  And fortunes tell, and read in loving bookes,
And thousand other wayes, to bait his fleshly hookes.

26

Inconstant man, that loved all he saw,
  And lusted after all, that he did love,
  Ne would his looser life be tide to law,   390
  But ioyd weake womens hearts to tempt and prove
  If from their loyall loves he might then move;
  Which lewdnesse fild him with reprochfull paine
  Of that fowle evill, which all men reprove,
  That rots the marrow, and consumes the braine: 395
Such one was *Lecherie*, the third of all this traine.

27

And greedy *Avarice* by him did ride,
  Upon a Camell loaden all with gold;
  Two iron coffers hong on either side,
  With precious mettall full, as they might hold,   400
  And in his lap an heape of coine he told;
  For of his wicked pelfe his God he made,
  And unto hell him selfe for money sold;
  Accursed usurie was all his trade,
And right and wrong ylike in equall ballaunce waide.   405

28

His life was nigh unto deaths doore yplast,
  And thred-bare cote, and cobled shoes he ware,
  Ne scarse good morsell all his life did tast,
  But both from backe and belly still did spare,
  To fill his bags, and richesse to compare;   410
  Yet chylde ne kinsman living had he none
  To leave them to; but thorough daily care
  To get, and nightly feare to lose his owne,
He led a wretched life unto him selfe unknowne.

29

Most wretched wight, whom nothing might suffise,⠀⠀⠀⠀415
⠀⠀Whose greedy lust did lacke in greatest store,
⠀⠀Whose need had end, but no end covetise,
⠀⠀Whose wealth was want, whose plenty made him pore,
⠀⠀Who had enough, yet wished ever more;
⠀⠀A vile disease, and eke in foote and hand⠀⠀⠀⠀420
⠀⠀A grievous gout tormented him full sore,
⠀⠀That well he could not touch, nor go, nor stand:
Such one was *Avarice*, the fourth of this faire band.

30

And next to him malicious *Envie* rode,
⠀⠀Upon a ravenous wolfe, and still did chaw⠀⠀⠀⠀425
⠀⠀Betweene his cankred teeth a venemous tode,
⠀⠀That all the poison ran about his chaw;
⠀⠀But inwardly he chawed his owne maw
⠀⠀At neighbours wealth, that made him ever sad;
⠀⠀For death it was, when any good he saw,⠀⠀⠀⠀430
⠀⠀And wept, that cause of weeping none he had,
But when he heard of harme, he wexed wondrous glad.

31

All in a kirtle of discolourd say
⠀⠀He clothed was, ypainted full of eyes;
⠀⠀And in his bosome secretly there lay⠀⠀⠀⠀435
⠀⠀An hatefull Snake, the which his taile uptyes
⠀⠀In many folds, and mortall sting implyes.
⠀⠀Still as he rode, he gnasht his teeth, to see
⠀⠀Those heapes of gold with griple Covetyse,
⠀⠀And grudged at the great felicitie⠀⠀⠀⠀440
Of proud *Lucifera*, and his owne companie.

32

He hated all good workes and vertuous deeds,
   And him no lesse, that any like did use,
   And who with gracious bread the hungry feeds,
   His almes for want of faith he doth accuse;   445
   So every good to bad he doth abuse:
   And eke the verse of famous Poets witt
   He does backebite, and spightfull poison spues
   From leprous mouth on all, that ever writt:
Such one vile *Envie* was, that fifte in row did sitt.   450

33

And him beside rides fierce revenging *Wrath*,
   Upon a Lion, loth for to be led;
   And in his hand a burning brond he hath,
   The which he brandisheth about his hed;
   His eyes did hurle forth sparkles fiery red,   455
   And stared sterne on all, that him beheld,
   As ashes pale of hew and seeming ded;
   And on his dagger still his hand he held,
Trembling through hasty rage, when choler in him sweld.

34

His ruffin raiment all was staind with blood,   460
   Which he had spilt, and all to rags yrent,
   Through unadvized rashnesse woxen wood;
   For of his hands he had no governement,
   Ne car'd for bloud in his avengement:
   But when the furious fit was overpast,   465
   His cruell facts he often would repent;
   Yet wilfull man he never would forecast,
How many mischieves should ensue his heedlesse hast.

35

Full many mischiefes follow cruell *Wrath*;
  Abhorred bloudshed, and tumultuous strife, 470
  Unmanly murder, and unthrifty scath,
  Bitter despight, with rancours rusty knife,
  And fretting griefe the enemy of life;
  All these, and many evils moe haunt ire,
  The swelling Splene, and Frenzy raging rife, 475
  The shaking Palsey, and Saint *Fraunces* fire:
Such one was *Wrath*, the last of this ungodly tire.

36

And after all, upon the wagon beame
  Rode *Sathan*, with a smarting whip in hand,
  With which he forward lasht the laesie teme, 480
  So oft as *Slowth* still in the mire did stand.
  Huge routs of people did about them band,
  Showting for joy, and still before their way
  A foggy mist had covered all the land;
  And underneath their feet, all scattered lay 485
Dead sculs and bones of men, whose life had gone astray.

37

So forth they marchen in this goodly sort,
  To take the solace of the open aire,
  And in fresh flowring fields themselves to sport;
  Emongst the rest rode that false Lady faire, 490
  The fowle *Duessa*, next unto the chaire
  Of proud *Lucifera*, as one of the traine:
  But that good knight would not so nigh repaire,
  Him selfe estraunging from their ioyaunce vaine,
Whose fellowship seemd far unfit for warlike swaine. 495

Fs

I. vii. 29–33

29

At last she chaunced by good hap to meet
  A goodly knight, faire marching by the way
  Together with his Squire, arayed meet:
  His glitterand armour shined farre away,
  Like glauncing light of *Phœbus* brightest ray;   500
  From top to toe no place appeared bare,
  That deadly dint of steele endanger may:
  Athwart his brest a bauldrick brave he ware,
That shynd, like twinkling stars, with stons most pretious
    rare.

30

And in the midst thereof one pretious stone   505
  Of wondrous worth, and eke of wondrous mights,
  Shapt like a Ladies head, exceeding shone,
  Like *Hesperus* emongst the lesser lights,
  And strove for to amaze the weaker sights;
  Thereby his mortall blade full comely hong   510
  In yvory sheath, ycarv'd with curious slights;
  Whose hilts were burnisht gold, and handle strong
Of mother pearle, and buckled with a golden tong.

31

His haughtie helmet, horrid all with gold,
  Both glorious brightnesse, and great terrour bred;   515
  For all the crest a Dragon did enfold
  With greedie pawes, and over all did spred
  His golden wings: his dreadfull hideous hed
  Close couched on the bever, seem'd to throw
  From flaming mouth bright sparkles fierie red,   520

That suddeine horror to faint harts did show;
And scaly tayle was stretcht adowne his backe full low.

32

Upon the top of all his loftie crest,
  A bunch of haires discolourd diversly,
    With sprincled pearle, and gold full richly drest,   525
  Did shake, and seem'd to daunce for iollity,
  Like to an Almond tree ymounted hye
  On top of greene *Selinis* all alone,
  With blossomes brave bedecked daintily;
    Whose tender locks do tremble every one   530
At every little breath, that under heaven is blowne.

33

His warlike shield all closely cover'd was,
  Ne might of mortall eye be ever seene;
  Not made of steele, nor of enduring bras,
    Such earthly mettals soone consumed bene: 535
  But all of Diamond perfect pure and cleene
  It framed was, one massie entire mould,
  Hewen out of Adamant rocke with engines keene,
  That point of speare it never percen could,
Ne dint of direfull sword divide the substance would.   540

I. ix. 45-54

45

Thou wretched man, of death hast greatest need,
  If in true ballance thou wilt weigh thy state:
  For never knight, that dared warlike deede.
  More lucklesse disaventures did amate:

Witnesse the dongeon deepe, wherein of late   545
　Thy life shut up, for death so oft did call;
　And though good lucke prolonged hath thy date,
　Yet death then, would the like mishaps forestall,
Into the which hereafter thou maiest happen fall.

46

Why then doest thou, O man of sin, desire   550
　To draw thy dayes forth to their last degree?
　Is not the measure of thy sinfull hire
　High heaped up with huge iniquitie,
　Against the day of wrath, to burden thee?
　Is not enough, that to this Ladie milde   555
　Thou falsed hast thy faith with periurie,
　And sold thy selfe to serve *Duessa* vilde,
With whom in all abuse thou hast thy selfe defilde?

47

Is not he iust, that all this doth behold
　From highest heaven, and beares an equall eye?   560
　Shell he thy sins up in his knowledge fold,
　And guiltie be of thine impietie?
　Is not his law, Let every sinner die:
　Die shall all flesh? what then must needs be donne,
　Is it not better to doe willinglie,   565
　Then linger, till the glasse be all out ronne?
Death is the end of woes: die soone, O faeries sonne.

48

The knight was much enmoved with his speach,
　That as a swords point through his hart did perse,
　And in his conscience made a secret breach,   570

Well knowing true all, that he did reherse
And to his fresh remembrance did reverse
The ugly vew of his deformed crimes,
That all his manly powres it did disperse,
As he were charmed with inchaunted rimes,   575
That oftentimes he quakt, and fainted oftentimes.

49

In which amazement, when the Miscreant
   Perceived him to waver weake and fraile,
   Whiles trembling horror did his conscience dant,
   And hellish anguish did his soule assaile,   580
   To drive him to despaire, and quite to quaile,
   He shew'd him painted in a table plaine,
   The damned ghosts, that doe in torments waile,
   And thousand feends that doe them endlesse paine
With fire and brimstone, which for ever shall remaine.   585

50

The sight whereof so throughly him dismaid,
   That nought but death before his eyes he saw,
   And ever burning wrath before him laid,
   By righteous sentence of th'Almighties law:
   Then gan the villein him to overcraw,   590
   And brought unto him swords, ropes, poison, fire,
   And all that might him to perdition draw;
   And bad him choose, what death he would desire:
For death was due to him, that had provokt Gods ire.

51

But when as none of them he saw him take,   595
   He to him raught a dagger sharpe and keene,

And gave it him in hand: his hand did quake,
And tremble like a leafe of Aspin greene,
And troubled bloud through his pale face was seene
To come, and goe with tydings from the hart,   600
As it a running messenger had beene.
At last resolv'd to worke his finall smart,
He lifted up his hand, that backe againe did start.

52
Which when as *Una* saw, through every vaine
    The crudled cold ran to her well of life,   605
    As in a swowne: but soone reliv'd againe,
    Out of his hand she snatcht the cursed knife,
    And threw it to the ground, enraged rife,
    And to him said, Fie, fie, faint harted knight,
    What meanest thou by this reprochfull strife?   610
    Is this the battell, which thou vauntst to fight
With that fire-mouthed Dragon, horrible and bright?

53
Come, come away, fraile, feeble, fleshly wight,
    Ne let vaine words bewitch thy manly hart,
    Ne divelish thoughts dismay thy constant spright.   615
    In heavenly mercies hast thou not a part?
    Why shouldst thou then despeire, that chosen art?
    Where iustice growes, there grows eke greater grace,
    The which doth quench the brond of hellish smart,
    And that accurst hand-writing doth deface.   620
Arise, Sir knight arise, and leave this cursed place.

54
So up he rose, and thence amounted streight.
    Which when the carle beheld, and saw his guest

Would safe depart, for all his subtill sleight,
He chose an halter from among the rest,   625
And with it hung himselfe, unbid unblest.
But death he could not worke himselfe thereby;
For thousand times he so himselfe had drest,
Yet nathelesse it could not doe him die,
Till he should die his last, that is eternally.   630

I. x. 46–68

46

Thence forward by that painfull way they pas,
    Forth to an hill, that was both steepe and hy.
    On top whereof a sacred chappell was,
    And eke a litle Hermitage thereby,
    Wherein an aged holy man did lye,   635
    That day and night said his devotion,
    Ne other worldly busines did apply;
    His name was heavenly *Contemplation*;
Of God and goodnesse was his meditation.

47

Great grace that old man to him given had;   640
    For God he often saw from heavens hight,
    All were his earthly eyen both blunt and bad,
    And through great age had lost their kindly sight,
    Yet wondrous quick and persant was his spright,
    As Eagles eye, that can behold the Sunne: 645
    That hill they scale with all their powre and might,
    That his frayle thighes nigh wearie and fordonne
Gan faile, but by her helpe the top at last he wonne.

48

There they do finde that godly aged Sire,
  With snowy lockes adowne his shoulders shed,   650
  As hoarie frost with spangles doth attire
  The mossy braunches of an Oke halfe ded.
  Each bone might through his body well be red,
  And every sinew seene through his long fast:
  For nought he car'd his carcas long unfed;   655
  His mind was full of spirituall repast,
And pyn'd his flesh, to keepe his body low and chast.

49

Who when these two approching he aspide,
  At their first presence grew agrieved sore,
  That forst him lay his heavenly thoughts aside;   660
  And had he not that Dame respected more,
  Whom highly he did reverence and adore,
  He would not once have moved for the knight.
  They him saluted standing far afore;
  Who well them greeting, humbly did requight,   665
And asked, to what end they clomb that tedious height.

50

What end (quoth she) should cause us take such paine,
  But that same end, which every living wight
  Should make his marke, high heaven to attaine?
  Is not from hence the way, that leadeth right   670
  To that most glorious house, that glistreth bright
  With burning starres, and everliving fire,
  Whereof the keyes are to thy hand behight
  By wise *Fidelia*? she doth thee require,
To shew it to this knight, according his desire.   675

51

Thrise happy man, said then the father grave,
   Whose staggering steps thy steady hand doth lead,
   And shewes the way, his sinfull soule to save.
   Who better can the way to heaven aread,
   Then thou thy selfe, that was both borne and bred   680
   In heavenly throne, where thousand Angels shine?
   Thou doest the prayers of the righteous sead
   Present before the maiestie divine,
And his avenging wrath to clemencie incline.

52

Yet since thou bidst, thy pleasure shalbe donne.   685
   Then come thou man of earth, and see the way,
   That never yet was seene of Faeries sonne,
   That never leads the traveiler astray,
   But after labours long, and sad delay,
   Brings them to ioyous rest and endlesse blis.   690
   But first thou must a season fast and pray,
   Till from her bands the spright assoiled is,
And have her strength recur'd from fraile infirmitis.

53

That done, he leads him to the highest Mount;
   Such one, as that same mighty man of God,   695
   That bloud-red billowes like a walled front
   On either side disparted with his rod,
   Till that his army dry-foot through them yod,
   Dwelt fortie dayes upon; where writ in stone
   With bloudy letters by the hand of God,   700
   The bitter doome of death and balefull mone
He did receive, whiles flashing fire about him shone.

54

Or like that sacred hill, whose head full hie,
   Adorned with fruitfull Olives all arownd,
   Is, as it were for endlesse memory   705
   Of that deare Lord, who oft thereon was fownd,
   For ever with a flowring girlond crownd:
   Or like that pleasaunt Mount, that is for ay
   Through famous Poets verse each where renownd,
   On which the thrise three learned Ladies play   710
Their heavenly notes, and make full many a lovely lay.

55

From thence, far off he unto him did shew
   A litle path, that was both steepe and long,
   Which to a goodly Citie led his vew;
   Whose wals and towres were builded high and strong 715
   Of perle and precious stone, that earthly tong
   Cannot describe, nor wit of man can tell;
   Too high a ditty for my simple song;
   The Citie of the great king hight it well,
Wherein eternall peace and happinesse doth dwell.   720

56

As he thereon stood gazing, he might see
   The blessed Angels to and fro descend
   From highest heaven, in gladsome companee,
   And with great ioy into that Citie wend,
   As commonly as friend does with his frend.   725
   Whereat he wondred much, and gan enquere,
   What stately building durst so high extend
   Her loftie towres unto the starry sphere,
And what unknowen nation there empeopled were.

57

Faire knight (quoth he) *Hierusalem* that is,   730
   The new *Hierusalem*, that God has built
   For those to dwell in, that are chosen his,
   His chosen people purg'd from sinfull guilt,
   With pretious bloud, which cruelly was spilt
   On cursed tree, of that unspotted lam,   735
   That for the sinnes of all the world was kilt:
   Now are they Saints all in that Citie sam,
More deare unto their God, then younglings to their dam.

58

Till now, said then the knight, I weened well,
   That great *Cleopolis*, where I have beene,   740
   In which that fairest *Faerie Queene* doth dwell,
   The fairest Citie was, that might be seene:
   And that bright towre all built of christall cleene,
   Panthea, seemd the brightest thing, that was:
   But now by proofe all otherwise I weene;   745
   For this great Citie that does far surpas,
And this bright Angels towre quite dims that towre of
   glas.

59

Most trew, then said the holy aged man;
   Yet is *Cleopolis* for earthly frame,
   The fairest peece, that eye beholden can: 750
   And well beseemes all knights of noble name,
   That covet in th'immortall booke of fame
   To be eternized, that same to haunt,
   And doen their service to that soveraigne Dame,
   That glorie does to them for guerdon graunt: 755
For she is heavenly borne, and heaven may iustly vaunt.

60

And thou faire ymp, sprong out from English race,
  How ever now accompted Elfins sonne,
  Well worthy doest thy service for her grace,
  To aide a virgin desolate foredonne.   760
  But when thou famous victorie hast wonne,
  And high emongst all knights hast hong thy shield,
  Thenceforth the suit of earthly conquest shonne,
  And wash thy hands from guilt of bloudy field:
For bloud can nought but sin, and wars but sorrowes   765
  yield.

61

Then seeke this path, that I to thee presage,
  Which after all to heaven shall thee send;
  Then peaceably thy painefull pilgrimage
  To yonder same *Hierusalem* do bend,
  Where is for thee ordaind a blessed end: 770
  For thou emongst those Saints, whom thou doest see,
  Shalt be a Saint, and thine owne nations frend
  And Patrone: thou Saint *George* shalt called bee,
Saint *George* of mery England, the signe of victoree.

62

Unworthy wretch (quoth he) of so great grace,   775
  How dare I thinke such glory to attaine?
  These that have it attaind, were in like cace
  (Quoth he) as wretched, and liv'd in like paine.
  But deeds of armes must I at last be faine,
  And Ladies love to leave so dearely bought?   780
  What need of armes, where peace doth ay remaine,
  (Said he) and battailes none are to be fought?
As for loose loves are vaine, and vanish into nought.

63

O let me not (quoth he) then turne againe
  Backe to the world, whose ioyes so fruitlesse are;   785
  But let me here for aye in peace remaine,
  Or streight way on that last long voyage fare,
  That nothing may my present hope empare.
  That may not be (said he) ne maist thou yit
  Forgo that royall maides bequeathed care,   790
  Who did her cause into thy hand commit,
Till from her cursed foe thou have her freely quit.

64

Then shall I soone, (quoth he) so God me grace,
  Abet that virgins cause disconsolate,
  And shortly backe returne unto this place   795
  To walke this way in Pilgrims poore estate.
  But now aread, old father, why of late
  Didst thou behight me borne of English blood,
  Whom all a Faeries sonne doen nominate?
  That word shall I (said he) avouchen good,   800
Sith to thee is unknowne the cradle of thy brood.

65

For well I wote, thou springst from ancient race
  Of *Saxon* kings, that have with mightie hand
  And many bloudie battailes fought in place
  High reard their royall throne in *Britane* land,   805
  And vanquisht them, unable to withstand:
  From thence a Faerie thee unweeting reft,
  There as thou slepst in tender swadling band,
  And her base Elfin brood there for thee left.
Such men do Chaungelings call, so chaungd by Faeries   810
    theft.

66

Thence she thee brought into this Faerie lond,
   And in an heaped furrow did thee hyde,
   Where thee a Ploughman all unweeting fond,
   As he his toylesome teme that way did guyde,
   And brought thee up in ploughmans state to byde,   815
   Whereof *Georgos* he thee gave to name;
   Till prickt with courage, and thy forces pryde,
   To Faery court thou cam'st to seeke for fame,
And prove thy puissaunt armes, as seemes thee best
    became.

67

O holy Sire (quoth he) how shall I quight   820
   The many favours I with thee have found,
   That hast my name and nation red aright,
   And taught the way that does to heaven bound?
   This said, adowne he looked to the ground,
   To have returnd, but dazed were his eyne,   825
   Through passing brightnesse, which did quite confound
   His feeble sence, and too exceeding shyne.
So darke are earthly things compard to things divine.

68

At last whenas himselfe he gan to find,
   To *Una* back he cast him to retire;   830
   Who him awaited still with pensive mind.
   Great thankes and goodly meed to that good syre,
   He thence departing gave for his paines hyre.
   So came to *Una*, who him ioyd to see,
   And after litle rest, gan him desire,   835
   Of her adventure mindfull for to bee.
So leave they take of *Cælia*, and her daughters three.

I. xi. 29–34, 46–48

29

It fortuned (as faire it then befell)
  Behind his backe unweeting, where he stood,
   Of auncient time there was a springing well,   840
   From which fast trickled forth a silver flood,
   Full of great vertues, and for med'cine good.
  Whylome, before that cursed Dragon got
  That happie land, and all with innocent blood
   Defyld those sacred waves, it rightly hot   845
The well of life, ne yet his vertues had forgot.

30

For unto life the dead it could restore,
  And guilt of sinfull crimes cleane wash away,
  Those that with sicknesse were infected sore,
  It could recure, and aged long decay   850
  Renew, as one were borne that very day.
  Both *Silo* this, and *Iordan* did excell,
  And th'English *Bath*, and eke the german *Spau*,
  Ne can *Cephise*, nor *Hebrus* match this well:
In the same the knight backe overthrowen, fell.   855

31

Now gan the golden *Phœbus* for to steepe
  His fierie face in billowes of the west,
  And his faint steedes watred in Ocean deepe,
  Whiles from their iournall labours they did rest,
  When that infernall Monster, having kest   860
  His wearie foe into that living well,
  Can high advance his broad discoloured brest,
  Above his wonted pitch, with countenance fell,
And clapt his yron wings, as victor he did dwell.

32

Which when his pensive Ladie saw from farre,   865
   Great woe and sorrow did her soule assay,
   As weening that the sad end of the warre,
   And gan to highest God entirely pray,
   That feared chance from her to turne away;
   With folded hands and knees full lowly bent   870
   All night she watcht, ne once adowne would lay
   Her daintie limbs in her sad dreriment,
But praying still did wake, and waking did lament.

33

The morrow next gan early to appeare,
   That *Titan* rose to runne his daily race;   875
   But early ere the morrow next gan reare
   Out of the sea faire *Titans* deawy face,
   Up rose the gentle virgin from her place,
   And looked all about, if she might spy
   Her loved knight to move his manly pace: 880
   For she had great doubt of his safety,
Since late she saw him fall before his enemy.

34

At last she saw, where he upstarted brave
   Out of the well, wherein he drenched lay;
   As Eagle fresh out of the Ocean wave,   885
   Where he hath left his plumes all hoary gray,
   And deckt himselfe with feathers youthly gay,
   Like Eyas hauke up mounts unto the skies,
   His newly budded pineons to assay,
   And marveiles at himselfe, still as he flies: 890
So new this new-borne knight to battell new did rise. . . .

46

There grew a goodly tree him faire beside,
  Loaden with fruit and apples rosie red,
  As they in pure vermilion had beene dide,
  Whereof great vertues over all were red: 895
  For happie life to all, which thereon fed,
  And life eke everlasting did befall:
  Great God it planted in that blessed sted
  With his almightie hand, and did it call
The tree of life, the crime of our first fathers fall.   900

47

In all the world like was not to be found,
  Save in that soile, where all good things did grow,
  And freely sprong out of the fruitfull ground,
  As incorrupted Nature did them sow,
  Till that dread Dragon all did overthrow.   905
  Another like faire tree eke grew thereby,
  Whereof who so did eat, eftsoones did know
  Both good and ill: O mornefull memory:
That tree through one mans fault hath doen us all to dy.

48

From that first tree forth flowd, as from a well,   910
  A trickling streame of Balme, most soveraine
  And daintie deare, which on the ground still fell,
  And overflowed all the fertill plaine,
  As it had deawed bene with timely raine:
  Life and long health that gratious ointment gave,   915
  And deadly woundes could heale, and reare againe
  The senselesse corse appointed for the grave.
Into that same he fell: which did from death him save.

  Gs

II. vii.

Guyon findes Mammon in a delve,
Sunning his threasure hore:
Is by him tempted, and led downe,
To see his secret store.

1

As Pilot well expert in perilous wave,
  That to a stedfast starre his course hath bent,   920
  When foggy mistes, or cloudy tempests have
  The faithfull light of that faire lampe yblent,
  And cover'd heaven with hideous dreriment,
  Upon his card and compas firmes his eye,
  The maisters of his long experiment,   925
  And to them does the steddy helme apply,
Bidding his winged vessell fairely forward fly:

2

So *Guyon* having lost his trusty guide,
  Late left beyond that *Ydle lake*, proceedes
  Yet on his way, of none accompanide;   930
  And evermore himselfe with comfort feedes,
  Of his owne vertues, and prayse-worthy deedes.
  So long he yode, yet no adventure found,
  Which fame of her shrill trompet worthy reedes:
  For still he traveild through wide wastfull ground,   935
That nought but desert wildernesse shew'd all around.

3

At last he came unto a gloomy glade,
  Cover'd with boughes and shrubs from heavens light,

Whereas he sitting found in secret shade
An uncouth, salvage, and uncivile wight,   940
Of griesly hew, and fowle ill favour'd sight;
His face with smoke was tand, and eyes were bleard,
His head and beard with sout were ill bedight,
His cole-blacke hands did seeme to have beene seard
In smithes fire-spitting forge, and nayles like clawes   945
    appeard.

4

His yron coate all overgrowne with rust,
    Was underneath enveloped with gold,
    Whose glistring glosse darkned with filthy dust,
    Well yet appeared, to have beene of old
    A worke of rich entayle, and curious mould,   950
    Woven with antickes and wild Imagery:
    And in his lap a masse of coyne he told,
    And turned upsidowne, to feede his eye
And covetous desire with his huge threasury.

5

And round about him lay on every side   955
    Great heapes of gold, that never could be spent:
    Of which some were rude owre, not purifide
    Of *Mulcibers* devouring element;
    Some others were new driven, and distent
    Into great Ingoes, and to wedges square;   960
    Some in round plates withouten moniment;
    But most were stampt, and in their metall bare
The antique shapes of kings and kesars straunge and
        rare.

6

Soone as he *Guyon* saw, in great affright
   And hast he rose, for to remove aside   965
   Those pretious hils from straungers envious sight.
   And downe them poured through an hole full wide,
   Into the hollow earth, them there to hide.
   But *Guyon* lightly to him leaping, stayd
   His hand, that trembled, as one terrifyde;   970
   And though him selfe were at the sight dismayd,
Yet him perforce restraynd, and to him doubtfull sayd.

7

What art thou man, (if man at all thou art)
   That here in desert hast thine habitaunce,
   And these rich heapes of wealth doest hide apart   975
   From the worldes eye, and from her right usaunce?
   Thereat with staring eyes fixed askaunce,
   In great disdaine, he answerd; Hardy Elfe,
   That darest vew my direfull countenaunce,
   I read thee rash, and heedlesse of thy selfe,   980
To trouble my still seate, and heapes of pretious pelfe.

8

God of the world and worldlings I me call,
   Great *Mammon*, greatest god below the skye,
   That of my plenty poure out unto all,
   And unto none my graces do envye: 985
   Riches, renowme, and principality,
   Honour, estate, and all this worldes good,
   For which men swinck and sweat incessantly,
   Fro me do flow into an ample flood,
And in the hollow earth have their eternall brood.   990

9

Wherefore if me thou deigne to serve and sew,
   At thy commaund lo all these mountaines bee;
   Or if to thy great mind, or greedy vew
   All these not suffise, there shall to thee
   Ten times so much be numbred francke and free.   995
   Mammon (said he) thy godheades vaunt is vaine,
   And idle offers of thy golden fee;
   To them, that covet such eye-glutting gaine,
Proffer thy giftes, and fitter servaunts entertaine.

10

Me ill besits. that in der-doing armes,   1000
   And honours suit my vowed dayes do spend,
   Unto thy bounteous baytes, and pleasing charmes,
   With which weake men thou witchest, to attend:
   Regard of worldly mucke doth fowly blend,
   And low abase the high heroicke spright,   1005
   That ioyes for crownes and kingdomes to contend;
   Faire shields, gay steedes, bright armes be my delight.
Those be the riches fit for an advent'rous knight.

11

Vaine glorious Elfe (said he) doest not thou weet,
   That money can thy wantes at will supply?   1010
   Sheilds, steeds, and armes, and all things for thee meet
   It can purvay in twinckling of an eye;
   And crownes and kingdomes to thee multiply.
   Do not I kings create, and throw the crowne
   Sometimes to him, that low in dust doth ly?   1015
   And him that raignd, into his rowme thrust downe,
And whom I lust, do heape with glory and renowne?

12

All otherwise (said he) I riches read,
  And deeme them roote of all disquietnesse;
  First got with guile, and then preserv'd with dread,   1020
  And after spent with pride and lavishnesse,
  Leaving behind them griefe and heavinesse.
  Infinite mischiefes of them do arize,
  Strife, and debate, bloudshed, and bitternesse,
  Outrageous wrong, and hellish covetize,   1025
That noble heart as great dishonour doth despize.

13

Ne thine be kingdomes, ne the scepters thine;
  But realmes and rulers thou doest both confound,
  And loyall truth to treason doest incline;
  Witnesse the guiltlesse bloud pourd oft on ground,   1030
  The crowned often slaine, the slayer cround,
  The sacred Diademe in peeces rent,
  And purple robe gored with many a wound;
  Castles surprizd, great cities sackt and brent:
So mak'st thou kings, and gaynest wrongfull governe- 1035
  ment.

14

Long were to tell the troublous stormes, that tosse
  The private state, and make the life unsweet:
  Who swelling sayles in Caspian sea doth crosse,
  And in frayle wood on *Adrian* gulfe doth fleet,
  Doth not, I weene, so many evils meet.   1040
  Then *Mammon* wexing wroth, And why then, said,
  Are mortall men so fond and undiscreet,
  So evill thing to seeke unto their ayd,
And having not complaine, and having it upbraid?

15

Indeede (quoth he) through fowle intemperaunce,　　1045
　　Frayle men are oft captiv'd to covetise:
　　But would they thinke, with how small allowaunce
Untroubled Nature doth her selfe suffise,
　　Such superfluities they would despise,
　　Which with sad cares empeach our native ioyes:　　1050
　　At the well head the purest streames arise:
　　But mucky filth his braunching armes annoyes,
And with uncomely weedes the gentle wave accloyes.

16

The antique world, in his first flowring youth,
　　Found no defect in his Creatours grace,　　1055
　　But with glad thankes, and unreproved truth,
　　The gifts of soveraigne bountie did embrace:
　　Like Angels life was then mens happy cace;
　　But later ages pride, like corn-fed steed,
　　Abusd her plenty, and fat swolne encrease　　1060
　　To all licentious lust, and gan exceed
The measure of her meane, and naturall first need.

17

Then gan a cursed hand the quiet wombe
　　Of his great Grandmother with steele to wound,
　　And the hid treasures in her sacred tombe,　　1065
　　With Sacriledge to dig.　Therein he found
　　Fountaines of gold and silver to abound,
　　Of which the matter of his huge desire
　　And pompous pride eftsoones he did compound;
　　Then avarice gan through his veines inspire　　1070
His greedy flames, and kindled life-devouring fire.

18

Sonne (said he then) let be thy bitter scorne,
    And leave the rudenesse of that antique age
    To them, that liv'd therein in state forlorne;
    Thou that doest live in later times, must wage   1075
    Thy workes for wealth, and life for gold engage.
    If then thee list my offred grace to use,
    Take what thou please of all this surplusage;
    If thee list not, leave have thou to refuse:
But thing refused, do not afterward accuse.   1080

19

Me list not (said the Elfin knight) receave
    Thing offred, till I know it well be got,
    Ne wote I, but thou didst these goods bereave
    From rightfull owner by unrighteous lot,
    Or that bloud guiltinesse or guile them blot.   1085
    Perdy (quoth he) yet never eye did vew,
    Ne toung did tell, ne hand these handled not,
    But safe I have them kept in secret mew,
From heavens sight, and powre of all which them pursew.

20

What secret place (quoth he) can safely hold   1090
    So huge a masse, and hide from heavens eye?
    Or where hast thou thy wonne, that so much gold
    Thou canst preserve from wrong and robbery?
    Come thou (quoth he) and see. So by and by
    Through that thicke covert he him led, and found   1095
    A darkesome way, which no man could descry,
    That deepe descended through the hollow ground,
And was with dread and horrour compassed around.

21

At length they came into a larger space,
   That stretcht it selfe into an ample plaine,   1100
   Through which a beaten broad high way did trace,
   That streight did lead to *Plutoes* griesly raine:
   By that wayes side, there sate infernall Payne,
   And fast beside him sat tumultuous Strife:
   The one in hand an yron whip did straine,   1105
   The other brandished a bloudy knife,
And both did gnash their teeth, and both did threaten life.

22

On thother side in one consort there sate,
   Cruell Revenge, and rancorous Despight,
   Disloyall Treason, and hart-burning Hate,   1110
   But gnawing Gealosie out of their sight
   Sitting alone, his bitter lips did bight,
   And trembling Feare still to and fro did fly,
   And found no place, where safe he shroud him might,
   Lamenting Sorrow did in darknesse lye,   1115
And Shame his ugly face did hide from living eye.

23

And over them sad Horrour with grim hew,
   Did alwayes sore, beating his yron wings;
   And after him Owles and Night-ravens flew
   The hatefull messengers of heavy things,   1120
   Of death and dolour telling sad tidings;
   Whiles sad *Celeno*, sitting on a clift,
   A song of bale and bitter sorrow sings,
   That hart of flint a sunder could have rift:
Which having ended, after him she flyeth swift.   1125

24

All these before the gates of *Pluto* lay,
  By whom they passing, spake unto them nought.
  But th'Elfin knight with wonder all the way
  Did feed his eyes, and fild his inner thought.
  At last him to a litle dore he brought,   1130
  That to the gate of Hell, which gaped wide,
  Was next adioyning, ne them parted ought:
  Betwixt them both was but a litle stride,
That did the house of Richesse from hell-mouth divide.

25

Before the dore sat selfe-consuming Care,   1135
  Day and night keeping wary watch and ward,
  For feare least Force or Fraud should unaware
  Breake in, and spoile the treasure there in gard:
  Ne would he suffer Sleepe once thither-ward
  Approch, albe his drowsie den were next;   1140
  For next to death is Sleep to be compard:
  Therefore his house is unto his annext;
Here Sleep, there Richesse, and Hel-gate them both
    betwext.

26

So soone as *Mammon* there arriv'd, the dore
  To him did open, and affoorded way;   1145
  Him followed eke Sir *Guyon* evermore,
  Ne darkenesse him, ne daunger might dismay.
  Soone as he entred was, the dore streight way
  Did shut, and from behind it forth there lept
  An ugly feend, more fowle then dismall day,   1150
  The which with monstrous stalke behind him stept,
And ever as he went, dew watch upon him kept.

27

Well hoped he, ere long that hardy guest,
  If ever covetous hand, or lustfull eye,
  Or lips he layd on thing, that likt him best,   1155
  Or ever sleepe his eye-strings did untye,
  Should be his pray.   And therefore still on hye
  He over him did hold his cruell clawes,
  Threatning with greedy gripe to do him dye
  And rend in peeces with his ravenous pawes,   1160
If ever he transgrest the fatail *Stygian* lawes.

28

That houses forme within was rude and strong,
  Like an huge cave, hewne out of rocky clift,
  From whose rough vaut the ragged breaches hong,
  Embost with massy gold of glorious gift,   1165
  And with rich metall loaded every rift,
  That heavy ruine they did seeme to threat;
  And over them *Arachne* high did lift
  Her cunning web, and spred her subtile net,
Enwrapped in fowle smoke and clouds more blacke   1170
  then Iet.

29

Both roofe, and floore, and wals were all of gold,
  But overgrowne with dust and old decay,
  And hid in darkenesse, that none could behold
  The hew thereof: for vew of chearefull day
  Did never in that house it selfe display,   1175
  But a faint shadow of uncertain light;
  Such as a lamp, whose life does fade away:
  Or as the Moone cloathed with clowdy night,
Does shew to him, that walkes in feare and sad affright.

30

In all that rowme was nothing to be seene,   1180
   But huge great yron chests and coffers strong,
   All bard with double bends, that none could weene
   Them to efforce by violence or wrong;
   On every side they placed were along.
   But all the ground with sculs was scattered,   1185
   And dead mens bones, which round about were flong,
   Whose lives, it seemed, whilome there were shed,
And their vile carcases now left unburied.

31

They forward passe, ne *Guyon* yet spoke word,
   Till that they came unto an yron dore,   1190
   Which to them opened of his owne accord,
   And shewd of richesse such exceeding store,
   As eye of man did never see before;
   Ne ever could within one place be found,
   Though all the wealth, which is, or was of yore,   1195
   Could gathered be through all the world around,
And that above were added to that under ground.

32

The charge thereof unto a covetous Spright
   Commaunded was, who thereby did attend,
   And warily awaited day and night,   1200
   From other covetous feends it to defend,
   Who it to rob and ransacke did intend.
   Then *Mammon* turning to that warriour, said;
   Loe here the worldes blis, loe here the end,
   To which all men do ayme, rich to be made: 1205
Such grace now to be happy, is before thee laid.

33

Certes (said he) I n'ill thine offred grace,
  Ne to be made so happy do intend:
  Another blis before mine eyes I place,
  Another happinesse, another end.   1210
    To them, that list, these base regardes I lend:
  But I in armes, and in atchievements brave,
  Do rather choose my flitting houres to spend,
  And to be Lord of those, that riches have,
Then them to have my selfe, and be their servile sclave.   1215

34

Thereat the feend his gnashing teeth did grate,
  And griev'd, so long to lacke his greedy pray;
  For well he weened, that so glorious bayte
  Would tempt his guest, to take thereof assay:
  Had he so doen, he had him snatcht away,   1220
  More light then Culver in the Faulcons fist.
  Eternall God thee save from such decay.
  But whenas *Mammon* saw his purpose mist,
Him to entrap unwares another way he wist.

35

Thence forward he him led, and shortly brought   1225
  Unto another rowme, whose dore forthright,
  To him did open, as it had beene taught:
  Therein an hundred raunges weren pight,
  And hundred fornaces all burning bright;
  By every fornace many feends did bide,   1230
  Deformed creatures, horrible in sight,
  And every feend his busie paines applide,
To melt the golden metall, ready to be tride.

36

One with great bellowes gathered filling aire,
    And with forst wind the fewell did inflame;   1235
    Another did the dying bronds repaire
    With yron toungs, and sprinkled oft the same
    With liquid waves, fiers *Vulcans* rage to tame,
    Who maistring them, renewd his former heat;
    Some scumd the drosse, that from the metall came;   1240
    Some stird the molten owre with ladles great;
And every one did swincke, and every one did sweat.

37

But when as earthly wight they present saw,
    Glistring in armes and battailous aray,
    From their whot worke they did themselves withdraw   1245
    To wonder at the sight: for till that day,
    They never creature saw, that came that way.
    Their staring eyes sparckling with fervent fire,
    And ugly shapes did nigh the man dismay,
    That were it not for shame, he would retire,   1250
Till that him thus bespake their soveraigne Lord and sire.

38

Behold, thou Faeries sonne, with mortall eye,
    That living eye before did never see:
    The thing, that thou didst crave so earnestly,
    To weet, whence all the wealth late shewd by mee,   1255
    Proceeded, lo now is reveald to thee.
    Here is the fountaine of the worldes good:
    Now therefore, if thou wilt enriched bee,
    Avise thee well, and chaunge thy wilfull mood,
Least thou perhaps hereafter wish, and be withstood.   1260

39

Suffise it then, thou Money God (quoth hee)
   That all thine idle offers I refuse.
   All that I need I have; what needeth mee
   To covet more, then I have cause to use?
   With such vaine shewes thy worldlings vile abuse: 1265
   But give me leave to follow mine emprise.
   Mammon was much displeasd, yet no'te he chuse,
   But beare the rigour of his bold mesprise,
And thence him forward led, him further to entise.

40

He brought him through a darksome narrow strait,   1270
   To a broad gate, all built of beaten gold:
   The gate was open, but therein did wait
   A sturdy villein, striding stiffe and bold,
   As if that highest God defie he would;
   In his right hand an yron club he held,   1275
   But he himselfe was all of golden mould,
   Yet had both life and sence, and well could weld
That cursed weapon, when his cruell foes he queld.

41

Disdayne he called was, and did disdaine
   To be so cald, and who so did him call: 1280
   Sterne was his looke, and full of stomacke vaine,
   His portaunce terrible, and stature tall,
   Far passing th'hight of men terrestriall;
   Like an huge Gyant of the *Titans* race,
   That made him scorne all creatures great and small,   1285
   And with his pride all others powre deface:
More fit amongst blacke fiendes, then men to have his
     place.

42

Soone as those glitterand armes he did espye,
    That with their brightnesse made that darknesse light,
    His harmefull club he gan to hurtle hye,   1290
    And threaten batteill to the Faery knight;
    Who likewise gan himselfe to batteill dight,
    Till *Mammon* did his hasty hand withhold,
    And counseld him abstaine from perilous fight:
    For nothing might abash the villein bold,   1295
Ne mortall steele emperce his miscreated mould.

43

So having him with reason pacifide,
    And the fiers Carle commaunding to forbeare,
    He brought him in. The rowme was large and wide,
    As it some Gyeld or solemne Temple weare: 1300
    Many great golden pillours did upbeare
    The massy roofe, and riches huge sustayne,
    And every pillour decked was full deare
    With crownes and Diademes, and titles vaine,
Which mortall Princes wore, whiles they on earth did   1305
    rayne.

44

A route of people there assembled were,
    Of every sort and nation under skye,
    Which with great uprore preaced to draw nere
    To th'upper part, where was advaunced hye
    A stately siege of soveraigne maiestye;   1310
    And thereon sat a woman gorgeous gay,
    And richly clad in robes of royaltye,
    That never earthly Prince in such aray
His glory did enhaunce, and pompous pride display.

45

Her face right wondrous faire did seeme to bee,   1315
  That her broad beauties beam great brightnes threw
  Through the dim shade, that all men might it see:
  Yet was not that same her owne native hew,
  But wrought by art and counterfetted shew,
  Thereby more lovers unto her to call;   1320
  Nath'lesse most heavenly faire in deed and vew
  She by creation was, till she did fall;
Thenceforth she sought for helps, to cloke her crime
    withall.

46

There, as in glistring glory she did sit,
  She held a great gold chaine ylincked well,   1325
  Whose upper end to highest heaven was knit,
  And lower part did reach to lowest Hell;
  And all that preace did round about her swell,
  To catchen hold of that long chaine, thereby
  To clime aloft, and others to excell: 1330
  That was *Ambition*, rash desire to sty,
And every lincke thereof a step of dignity.

47

Some thought to raise themselves to high degree,
  By riches and unrighteous reward,
  Some by close shouldring, some by flatteree;   1335
  Others through friends, others for base regard;
  And all by wrong wayes for themselves prepard.
  Those that were up themselves, kept others low,
  Those that were low themselves, held others hard,
  Ne suffred them to rise or greater grow,   1340
But every one did strive his fellow downe to throw.
  Hs

48

Which whenas *Guyon* saw, he gan inquire,
  What meant that preace about that Ladies throne,
  And what she was that did so high aspire.
  Him *Mammon* answered; That goodly one,   1345
  Whom all that folke with such contention,
  Do flocke about, my deare, my daughter is;
  Honour and dignitie from her alone
  Derived are, and all this worldes blis
For which ye men do strive: few get, but many mis.   1350

49

And faire *Philotime* she rightly hight,
  The fairest wight that wonneth under skye,
  But that this darksome neather world her light
  Doth dim with horrour and deformitie,
  Worthy of heaven and hye felicitie,   1355
  From whence the gods have her for envy thrust:
  But sith thou hast found favour in mine eye,
  Thy spouse I will her make, if that thou lust,
That she may thee advance for workes and merites iust.

50

Gramercy *Mammon* (said the gentle knight)   1360
  For so great grace and offred high estate;
  But I, that am fraile flesh and earthly wight,
  Unworthy match for such immortall mate
  My selfe well wote, and mine unequall fate;
  And were I not, yet is my trouth yplight,   1365
  And love avowd to other Lady late,
  That to remove the same I have no might:
To chaunge love causelesse is reproch to warlike knight.

51

Mammon emmoved was with inward wrath;
  Yet forcing it to faine, him forth thence led   1370
  Through griesly shadowes by a beaten path,
  Into a gardin goodly garnished
  With hearbs and fruits, whose kinds mote not be red:
  Not such, as earth out of her fruitfull woomb
  Throwes forth to men, sweet and well savoured,   1375
  But direfull deadly blacke both leafe and bloom,
Fit to adorne the dead, and decke the drery toombe.

52

There mournfull *Cypresse* grew in greatest store,
  And trees of bitter *Gall*, and *Heben* sad,
  Dead sleeping *Poppy*, and blacke *Hellebore*,   1380
  Cold *Coloquintida*, and *Tetra* mad,
  Mortall *Samnitis*, and *Cicuta* bad,
  With which th'uniust *Atheniens* made to dy
  Wise *Socrates*, who thereof quaffing glad
  Pourd out his life, and last Philosophy   1385
To the faire *Critias* his dearest Belamy.

53

The *Gardin* of *Proserpina* this hight;
  And in the midst thereof a silver seat,
  With a thicke Arber goodly over dight,
  In which she often usd from open heat   1390
  Her selfe to shroud, and pleasures to entreat.
  Next thereunto did grow a goodly tree,
  With braunches broad dispred and body great,
  Clothed with leaves, that none the wood mote see
And loaden all with fruit as thicke as it might bee.   1395

54

Their fruit were golden apples glistring bright,
   That goodly was their glory to behold,
   On earth like never grew, ne living wight
   Like ever saw, but they from hence were sold:
   For those, which *Hercules* with conquest bold   1400
   Got from great *Atlas* daughters, hence began,
   And planted there, did bring forth fruit of gold:
   And those with which the'*Eubæan* young man wan
Swift *Atalanta*, when through craft he her out ran.

55

Here also sprong that goodly golden fruit,   1405
   With which *Acontius* got his lover trew,
   Whom he had long time sought with fruitlesse suit:
   Here eke that famous golden Apple grew,
   The which emongst the gods false *Ate* threw;
   For which th'*Idæan* Ladies disagreed,   1410
   Till partiall *Paris* dempt it *Venus* dew,
   And had of her, faire *Helen* for his meed,
That many noble *Greekes* and *Troians* made to bleed.

56

The warlike Elfe much wondred at this tree,
   So faire and great, that shadowed all the ground,   1415
   And his broad braunches, laden with rich fee,
   Did stretch themselves without the utmost bound
   Of this great gardin, compast with a mound,
   Which over-hanging, they themselves did steepe,
   In a blacke flood which flow'd about it round;   1420
   That is the river of *Cocytus* deepe,
In which full many soules do endlesse waile and weepe.

57

Which to behold, he clomb up to the banke,
  And looking downe, saw many damned wights,
  In those sad waves, which direfull deadly stanke,   1425
  Plonged continually of cruell Sprights,
  That with their pitteous cryes, and yelling shrights,
  They made the further shore resounden wide:
  Emongst the rest of those same ruefull sights,
  One cursed creature he by chaunce espide,   1430
That drenched lay full deepe, under the Garden side.

58

Deepe was he drenched to the upmost chin,
  Yet gaped still, as coveting to drinke
  Of the cold liquor, which he waded in,
  And stretching forth his hand, did often thinke   1435
  To reach the fruit, which grew upon the brincke:
  But both the fruit from hand, and floud from mouth
  Did flie abacke, and made him vainely swinke:
  The whiles he sterv'd with hunger and with drouth
He daily dyde, yet never throughly dyen couth.   1440

59

The knight him seeing labour so in vaine,
  Askt who he was, and what he ment thereby:
  Who groning deepe, thus answerd him againe;
  Most cursed of all creatures under skye,
  Lo *Tantalus*, I here tormented lye: 1445
  Of whom high *Iove* wont whylome feasted bee,
  Lo here I now for want of food doe dye:
  But if that thou be such, as I thee see,
Of grace I pray thee, give to eat and drinke to mee.

60

Nay, nay, thou greedie *Tantalus* (quoth he)   1450
  Abide the fortune of thy present fate,
  And unto all that live in high degree,
  Ensample be of mind intemperate,
  To teach them how to use their present state.
  Then gan the cursed wretch aloud to cry,   1455
  Accusing highest *Iove* and gods ingrate,
  And eke blaspheming heaven bitterly,
As authour of uniustice, there to him dye.

61

He lookt a little further, and espyde
  Another wretch, whose carkasse deepe was drent   1460
  Within the river, which the same did hyde:
  But both his hands most filthy feculent,
  Above the water were on high extent,
  And faynd to wash themselves incessantly;
  Yet nothing cleaner were for such intent,   1465
  But rather fowler seemed to the eye;
So lost his labour vaine and idle industry.

62

The knight him calling, asked who he was,
  Who lifting up his head, him answerd thus:
  I *Pilate* am the falsest Iudge, alas,   1470
  And most uniust, that by unrighteous
  And wicked doome, to Iewes despiteous
  Delivered up the Lord of life to die,
  And did acquite a murdrer felonous;
  The whiles my hands I washt in puritie,   1475
The whiles my soule was soyld with foule iniquitie.

63

Infinite moe, tormented in like paine
  He there beheld, too long here to be told:
  Ne *Mammon* would there let him long remaine,
  For terrour of the tortures manifold,   1480
  In which the damned soules he did behold,
  But roughly him bespake. Thou fearefull foole,
  Why takest not of that same fruit of gold,
  Ne sittest downe on that same silver stoole,
To rest thy wearie person, in the shadow coole.   1485

64

All which he did, to doe him deadly fall
  In frayle intemperance through sinfull bayt;
  To which if he inclined had at all,
  That dreadfull feend, which did behind him wayt,
  Would him have rent in thousand peeces strayt: 1490
  But he was warie wise in all his way,
  And well perceived his deceiptfull sleight,
  Ne suffred lust his safetie to betray;
So goodly did beguile the Guyler of the pray.

65

And now he has so long remained there,   1495
  That vitall powres gan wexe both weake and wan,
  For want of food, and sleepe, which two upbeare,
  Like mightie pillours, this fraile life of man,
  That none without the same enduren can.
  For now three dayes of men were full out-wrought,   1500
  Since he this hardie enterprize began:
  For thy great *Mammon* fairely he besought,
Into the world to guide him backe, as he him brought.

66

The God, though loth, yet was constraind t'obay,
  For lenger time, then that, no living wight   1505
  Below the earth, might suffred be to stay:
  So backe againe, him brought to living light.
  But all so soone as his enfeebled spright
  Gan sucke this vitall aire into his brest,
  As overcome with too exceeding might,   1510
  The life did flit away out of her nest,
And all his senses were with deadly fit opprest.

II. xii. 70–87

70

Eftsoones they heard a most melodious sound,
  Of all that mote delight a daintie eare,
  Such as attone might not on living ground,   1515
  Save in this Paradise, be heard elswhere:
  Right hard it was, for wight, which did it heare,
  To read, what manner musicke that mote bee:
  For all that pleasing is to living eare,
  Was there consorted in one harmonee,   1520
Birdes, voyces, instruments, windes, waters, all agree.

71

The ioyous birdes shrouded in chearefull shade,
  Their notes unto the voyce attempred sweet;
  Th'Angelicall soft trembling voyces made
  To th'instruments divine respondence meet: 1525
  The silver sounding instruments did meet
  With the base murmure of the waters fall:
  The waters fall with difference discreet,
  Now soft, now loud, unto the wind did call:
The gentle warbling wind low answered to all.   1530

72

There, whence that Musick seemed heard to bee,
    Was the faire Witch her selfe now solacing,
    With a new Lover, whom through sorceree
    And witchcraft, she from farre did thither bring:
    There she had him now layd a slombering,   1535
    In secret shade, after long wanton ioyes:
    Whilst round about them pleasauntly did sing
    Many faire Ladies, and lascivious boyes,
That ever mixt their song with light licentious toyes.

73

And all that while, right over him she hong,   1540
    With her false eyes fast fixed in his sight,
    As seeking medicine, whence she was stong,
    Or greedily depasturing delight:
    And oft inclining downe with kisses light,
    For feare of waking him, his lips bedewd,   1545
    And through his humid eyes did sucke his spright,
    Quite molten into lust and pleasure lewd;
Wherewith she sighed soft, as if his case she rewd.

74

The whiles some one did chaunt this lovely lay;
    Ah see, who so faire thing doest faine to see,   1550
    In springing flowre the image of thy day;
    Ah see the Virgin Rose, how sweetly shee
    Doth first peepe forth with bashfull modestee,
    That fairer seemes, the lesse ye see her may;
    Lo see soone after, how more bold and free   1555
    Her bared bosome she doth broad display;
Loe see soone after, how she fades, and falles away.

75

Sy passeth, in the passing of a day,
    Of mortall life the leafe, the bud, the flowre,
    Ne more doth flourish after first decay,   1560
That earst was sought to decke both bed and bowre,
    Of many a Ladie, and many a Paramowre:
    Gather therefore the Rose, whilest yet is prime,
    For soone comes age, that will her pride deflowre:
    Gather the Rose of love, whilest yet is time,   1565
Whilest loving thou mayst loved be with equall crime.

76

He ceast, and then gan all the quire of birdes
    Their diverse notes t'attune unto his lay,
    As in approvance of his pleasing words.
    The constant paire heard all, that he did say,   1570
    Yet swarved not, but kept their forward way,
    Through many covert groves, and thickets close,
    In which they creeping did at last display
    That wanton Ladie, with her lover lose,
Whose sleepie head she in her lap did soft dispose.   1575

77

Upon a bed of Roses she was layd,
    As faint through heat, or dight to pleasant sin,
    And was arayd, or rather disarayd,
    All in a vele of silke and silver thin,
    That hid not whit her alablaster skin,   1580
    But rather shewd more white, if more might bee:
    More subtile web *Arachne* cannot spin,
    Nor the fine nets, which ofte we woven see
Of scorched deaw, do not in the'aire more lightly flee.

78

Her snowy brest was bare to readie spoyle   1585
  Of hungry eies, which n'ote therewith be fild,
  And yet through languour of her late sweet toyle,
  Few drops, more cleare then Nectar, forth distild,
  That like pure Orient perles adowne it trild
  And her faire eyes sweet smyling in delight,   1590
  Moystened their fierie beames, with which she thrild
  Fraile harts, yet quenched not; like starry light
Which sparckling on the silent waves, does seeme more
    bright.

79

The young man sleeping by her, seemd to bee
  Some goodly swayne of honorable place,   1595
  That certes it great pittie was to see
  Him his nobilitie so foule deface;
  A sweet regard, and amiable grace,
  Mixed with manly sternnesse did appeare
  Yet sleeping, in his well proportiond face,   1600
  And on his tender lips the downy heare
Did now but freshly spring, and silken blossomes beare.

80

His warlike armes, the idle instruments
  Of sleeping praise, were hong upon a tree,
  And his brave shield, full of old moniments,   1605
  Was fowly ra'st, that none the signes might see;
  Ne for them, ne for honour cared hee,
  Ne ought, that did to his advauncement tend,
  But in lewd loves, and wastfull luxuree,
  His dayes, his goods, his bodie he did spend: 1610
O horrible enchantment, that him so did blend.

81

The noble Elfe, and carefull Palmer drew
   Sonigh them, minding nought, but lustfull game,
   That suddein forth they on them rusht, and threw
   A subtile net, which onely for the same   1615
   The skillfull Palmer formally did frame.
   So held them under fast, the whiles the rest
   Fled all away for feare of fowler shame.
   The faire Enchauntresse, so unwares opprest,
Tryde all her arts, and all her sleights, thence out to wrest. 1620

82

And eke her lover strove: but all in vaine;
   For that same net so cunningly was wound,
   That neither guile, nor force might it distraine.
   They tooke them both, and both them strongly bound
   In captive bandes, which there they readie found: 1625
   But her in chaines of adamant he tyde;
   For nothing else might keepe her safe and sound;
   But *Verdant* (so he hight) he soone untyde,
And counsell sage in steed thereof to him applyde.

83

But all those pleasant bowres and Pallace brave,   1630
   Guyon broke downe, with rigous pittilesse;
   Ne ought their goodly workmanship might save
   Them from the tempest of his wrathfulnesse,
   But that their blisse he turn'd to balefulnesse:
   Their groves he feld, their gardins did deface,   1635
   Their arbers spoyle, their Cabinets suppresse,
   Their banket houses burne, their buildings race,
And of the fairest late, now made the fowlest place.

84

Then led they her away, and eke that knight
  They with them led, both sorrowfull and sad: 1640
  The way they came, the same retourn'd they right,
  Till they arrived, where they lately had
  Charm'd those wild-beasts, that rag'd with furie mad.
  Which now awaking, fierce at them gan fly,
  As in their mistresse reskew, whom they lad; 1645
  But them the Palmer soone did pacify.
Then *Guyon* askt, what meant those beastes, which there
    did ly.

85

Said he, These seeming beasts are men indeed,
  Whom this Enchauntresse hath transformed thus,
  Whylome her lovers, which her lusts did feed, 1650
  Now turned into figures hideous,
  According to their mindes like monstruous.
  Sad end (quoth he) of life intemperate,
  And mournefull meed of ioyes delicious:
  But Palmer, if it mote thee so aggrate, 1655
Let them returned be unto their former state.

86

Streight way he with his vertuous staffe them strooke,
  And streight of beasts they comely men became;
  Yet being men they did unmanly looke,
  And stared ghastly, some for inward shame, 1660
  And some for wrath, to see their captive Dame:
  But one above the rest in speciall,
  That had an hog beene late, hight *Grille* by name,
  Repined greatly, and did him miscall,
That had from hoggish forme him brought to naturall. 1665

87

Said *Guyon*, See the mind of beastly man,
   That hath so soone forgot the excellence
   Of his creation, when he life began,
   That now he chooseth, with vile difference,
   To be a beast, and lacke intelligence.   1670
   To whom the Palmer thus, The donghill kind
   Delights in filth and foule incontinence:
   Let *Grill* be *Grill*, and have his hoggish mind,
But let us hence depart, whilest wether serves and wind.

III. vi. 26–52

26

To search the God of love, her Nymphes she sent   1675
   Throughout the wandring forrest every where:
   And after them her selfe eke with her went
   To seeke the fugitive, both farre and nere,
   So long they sought, till they arrived were
   In that same shadie covert, whereas lay   1680
   Faire *Crysogone* in slombry traunce whilere:
   Who in her sleepe (a wondrous thing to say)
Unwares had borne two babes, as faire as springing day.

27

Unwares she them conceiv'd, unwares she bore:
   She bore withouten paine, that she conceived   1685
   Withouten pleasure: ne her need implore
   Lucinaes aide: which when they both perceived,
   They were through wonder nigh of sense bereaved,
   And gazing each on other, nought bespake:
   At last they both agreed, her seeming grieved   1690
   Out of her heavy swowne not to awake,
But from her loving side the tender babes to take.

28

Up they them tooke, each one a babe uptooke,
  And with them carried, to be fostered;
  Dame *Phœbe* to a Nymph her babe betooke,   1695
  To be upbrought in perfect Maydenhed,
  And of her selfe her name *Belphœbe* red:
  But *Venus* hers thence farre away convayd,
  To be upbrought in goodly womanhed,
  And in her litle loves stead, which was strayd,   1700
Her *Amoretta* cald, to comfort her dismayd.

29

She brought her to her ioyous Paradize,
  Where most she wonnes, when she on earth does dwel.
  So faire a place, as Nature can devize:
  Whether in *Paphos*, or *Cytheron* hill,   1705
  Or it in *Gnidus* be, I wote not well;
  But well I wote by tryall, that this same
  All other pleasant places doth excell,
  And called is by her lost lovers name
The *Gardin* of *Adonis*, farre renowmd by fame.   1710

30

In that same Gardin all the goodly flowres,
  Wherewith dame Nature doth her beautifie,
  And decks the girlonds of her paramoures,
  Are fetcht: there is the first seminarie
  Of all things, that are borne to live and die,   1715
  According to their kindes. Long worke it were,
  Here to account the endlesse progenie
  Of all the weedes, that bud and blossome there;
But so much as doth need, must needs be counted here.

31

It sited was in fruitfull soyle of old,   1720
   And girt in with two walles on either side;
   The one of yron, the other of bright gold,
   That none might thorough breake, nor overstride:
   And double gates it had, which opened wide,
   By which both in and out men moten pas;   1725
   Th'one faire and fresh, the other old and dride:
   Old *Genius* the porter of them was,
Old *Genius*, the which a double nature has.

32

He letteth in, he letteth out to wend,
   All that to come into the world desire;   1730
   A thousand thousand naked babes attend
   About him day and night, which doe require,
   That he with fleshly weedes would them attire:
   Such as him list, such as eternall fate
   Ordained hath, he clothes with sinfull mire,   1735
   And sendeth forth to live in mortall state,
Till they againe returne backe by the hinder gate.

33

After that they againe returned beene,
   They in that Gardin planted be againe;
   And grow afresh, as they had never seene   1740
   Fleshly corruption, nor mortall paine.
   Some thousand yeares so doen they there remaine;
   And then of him are clad with other hew,
   Or sent into the chaungefull world againe,
   Till thither they returne, where first they grew: 1745
So like a wheele around they runne from old to new.

34

Ne needs there Gardiner to set, or sow,
  To plant or prune: for of their owne accord
  All things, as they created were, doe grow,
  And yet remember well the mightie word,   1750
  Which first was spoken by th'Almightie lord,
  That bad them to increase and multiply:
  Ne doe they need with water of the ford,
  Or of the clouds to moysten their roots dry;
For in themselves eternall moisture they imply.   1755

35

Infinite shapes of creatures there are bred,
  And uncouth formes, which none yet ever knew,
  And every sort is in a sundry bed
  Set by it selfe, and ranckt in comely rew:
  Some fit for reasonable soules t'indew,   1760
  Some made for beasts, some made for birds to weare,
  And all the fruitfull spawne of fishes hew
  In endlesse rancks along enraunged were,
That seem'd the *Ocean* could not containe them there.

36

Daily they grow, and daily forth are sent   1765
  Into the world, it to replenish more;
  Yet is the stocke not lessened, nor spent,
  But still remaines in everlasting store,
  As it at first created was of yore,
  For in the wide wombe of the world there lyes,   1770
  In hatefull darkenesse and in deepe horrore,
  An huge eternall *Chaos*, which supplyes
The substances of natures fruitfull progenyes.

  Is

37

All things from thence doe their first being fetch,
 And borrow matter, whereof they are made,   1775
 Which when as forme and feature it does ketch,
 Becomes a bodie, and doth then invade
 The state of life, out of the griesly shade.
 That substance is eterne, and bideth so,
 Ne when the life decayes, and forme does fade, 1780
 Doth it consume, and into nothing go,
But chaunged is, and often altred to and fro.

38

The substance is not chaunged, nor altered,
 But th'only forme and outward fashion;
 For every substance is conditioned   1785
 To change her hew, and sundry formes to don,
 Meet for her temper and complexion:
 For formes are variable and decay,
 By course of kind, and by occasion;
 And that faire flowre of beautie fades away, 1790
As doth the lilly fresh before the sunny ray.

39

Great enimy to it, and to all the rest,
 That in the *Gardin* of *Adonis* springs,
 Is wicked *Time*, who with his scyth addrest.
 Does mow the flowring herbes and goodly things, 1795
 And all their glory to the ground downe flings,
 Where they doe wither, and are fowly mard:
 He flyes about, and with his flaggy wings.
 Beates downe both leaves and buds without regard,
 Ne ever pittie may relent his malice hard. 1800

40

Yet pittie often did the gods relent,
  To see so faire things mard, and spoyled quight:
  And their great mother *Venus* did lament
  The losse of her deare brood, her deare delight:
  Her hart was pierst with pittie at the sight,   1805
  When walking through the Gardin, them she spyde,
  Yet no'te she find redresse for such despight.
  For all that lives, is subiect to that law:
All things decay in time, and to their end do draw,

41

But were it not, that *Time* their troubler is,   1810
  All that in this delightfull Gardin growes,
  Should happie be, and have immortall blis.
  For here all plentie, and all pleasure flowes,
  And sweet love gentle fits emongst them throwes,
  Without fell rancor, or fond gealosie;   1815
  Franckly each paramour his leman knowes.
  Each bird his mate, ne any does envie
Their goodly meriment, and gay felicitie.

42

There is continuall spring, and harvest there
  Continuall, both meeting at one time: 1820
  For both the boughes doe laughing blossomes beare,
  And with fresh colours decke the wanton Prime,
  And eke attonce the heavy trees they clime,
  Which seeme to labour under their fruits lode:
  The whiles the ioyous birdes make their pastime   1825
  Emongst the shadie leaves, their sweet abode,
And their true loves without suspition tell abrode.

43

Right in the midddest of that Paradise,
  There stood a stately Mount, on whose round top
  A gloomy grove of mirtle trees did rise,   1830
  Whose shadie boughes sharpe steele did never lop,
  Nor wicked beasts their tender buds did crop,
  But like a girlond compassed the hight,
  And from their fruitfull sides sweet gum did drop,
  That all the ground with precious deaw bedight,   1835
Threw forth most dainty odours, and most sweet delight.

44

And in the thickest covert of that shade,
  There was a pleasant arbour, not by art.
  But of the trees owne inclination made,
  Which knitting their rancke braunches part to part,   1840
  With wanton yuie twyne entrayld athwart,
  And Eglantine, and Caprifole emong,
  Fashiond above within their inmost part,
  That nether *Phœbus* beams could through them throng,
Nor *Aeolus* sharp blast could worke them any wrong.   1845

45

And all about grew every sort of flowre,
  To which sad lovers were transformd of yore;
  Fresh *Hyacinthus*, *Phœbus* paramoure,
  And dearest love,
  Foolish *Narcisse*, that likes the watry shore,   1850
  Sad *Amaranthus*, made a flowre but late,
  Sad *Amaranthus*, in whose purple gore
  Me seemes I see *Amintas* wretched fate,
To whom sweet Poets verse hath given endlesse date.

46

There wont faire *Venus* often to enioy   1855
   Her deare *Adonis* ioyous company,
   And reape sweet pleasure of the wanton boy;
   There yet, some say, in secret he does ly,
   Lapped in flowres and pretious spycery,
   By her hid from the world, and from the skill   1860
   Of *Stygian* Gods, which doe her love envy;
   But she her selfe, when ever that she will,
Possesseth him, and of his sweetnesse takes her fill.

47

And sooth it seemes they say: for he may not
   For ever die, and ever buried bee   1865
   In balefull night, where all things are forgot;
   All be he subiect to mortalitie,
   Yet is eterne in mutabilitie,
   And by succession made perpetuall,
   Transformed oft, and chaunged diverslie: 1870
   For him the Father of all formes, they call;
Therefore needs mote he live, that living gives to all.

48

There now he liveth in eternall blis,
   Ioying his goddesse, and of her enioyd:
   Ne feareth he henceforth that foe of his,   1875
   Which with his cruell tuske him deadly cloyd:
   For that wilde Bore, the which him once annoyd,
   She firmely hath emprisoned for ay,
   That her sweet love his malice mote avoyd,
   In a strong rocky Cave, which is they say,   1880
Hewen underneath that Mount, that none him losen may.

49

There now he lives in everlasting ioy,
   With many of the Gods in company,
   Which thither haunt, and with the winged boy
   Sporting himselfe in safe felicity: 1885
   Who when he hath with spoiles and cruelty
   Ransackt the world, and in the wofull harts
   Of many wretches set his triumphes hye,
   Thither resorts, and laying his sad darts
Aside, with faire *Adonis* playes his wanton parts.   1890

50

And his true love faire *Psyche* with him playes,
   Faire *Psyche* to him lately reconcyld,
   After long troubles and unmeet upbrayes,
   With which his mother *Venus* her revyld,
   And eke himselfe her cruelly exyld: 1895
   But now in stedfast love and happy state
   She with him lives, and hath him borne a chyld,
   Pleasure, that doth both gods and men aggrate,
Pleasure, the daughter of *Cupid* and *Psyche* late.

51

Hither great *Venus* brought this infant faire.   1900
   The younger daughter of *Chrysogonee*,
   And unto *Psyche* with great trust and care
   Committed her, yfostered to bee,
   And trained up in true feminitee:
   Who no lesse carefully her tendered,   1905
   Then her owne daughter *Pleasure*, to whom shee
   Made her companion, and her lessoned
In all the lore of love, and goodly womanhead.

52

In which when she to perfect ripenesse grew,
   Of grace and beautie noble Paragone,   1910
   She brought her forth into the worldes vew,
   To be th'ensample of true love alone,
   And Lodestarre of all chaste affectione,
   To all faire Ladies, that doe live on ground.
   To Faery court she came, where many one   1915
   Admyred her goodly haveour, and found
His feeble hart wide launched with loves cruell wound.

IV. x. 23–52

23

In such luxurious plentie of all pleasure,
   It seem'd a second paradise to ghesse,
   So lavishly enricht with natures threasure,   1920
   That if the happie soules, which doe possesse
   Th'Elysian fields, and live in lasting blesse,
   Should happen this with living eye to see,
   They soone would loath their lesser happinesse
   And wish to life return'd againe to bee,   1925
That in this ioyous place they mote have ioyance free.

24

Fresh shadowes, fit to shroud from sunny ray;
   Faire lawnds, to take the sunne in season dew;
   Sweet springs, in which a thousand Nymphs did play;
   Soft rombling brookes, that gentle slomber drew;   1930
   High reared mounts, the lands about to vew;
   Low looking dales, disloignd from common gaze;
   Delightfull bowres, to solace lovers trew;
   False Labyrinthes, fond runners eyes to daze;
All which by nature made did nature selfe amaze.   1935

25

And all without were walkes and alleyes dight
  With divers trees, enrang'd in even rankes;
  And here and there were pleasant arbors pight.
  And shadie seates, and sundry flowring bankes,
  To sit and rest the walkers wearie shankes,   1940
  And therein thousand payres of lovers walkt,
  Praysing their god, and yeelding him great thankes,
  Ne ever ought but of their true loves talkt,
Ne ever for rebuke or blame of any balkt.

26

All these together by themselves did sport   1945
  Their spotlesse pleasures, and sweet loves content.
  But farre away from these, another sort
  Of lovers lincked in true harts consent;
  Which loved not as these, for like intent,
  But on chast vertue grounded their desire,   1950
  Farre from all fraud, or fayned blandishment;
  Which in their spirits kindling zealous fire,
Brave thoughts and noble deedes did evermore aspire.

27

Such were great *Hercules*, and *Hylas* deare;
  Trew *Ionathan*, and *David* trustie tryde;   1955
  Stout *Theseus*, and *Pirithous* his feare;
  Pylades and *Orestes* by his syde;
  Myld *Titus* and *Gesippus* without pryde;
  Damon and *Pythias* whom death could not sever:
  All these and all that ever had bene tyde   1960
  In bands of friendship, there did live for ever,
Whose lives although decay'd, yet loves decayed never.

28

Which when as I, that never tasted blis,
  Nor happie howre, beheld with gazefull eye,
  I thought there was none other heaven then this;   1965
  And gan their endlesse happinesse envye,
  That being free from feare and gealosye,
  Might frankely there their loves desire possesse;
  Whilest I through paines and perlous ieopardie,
  Was forst to seeke my lifes deare patronesse: 1970
Much dearer be the things, which come through hard
    distresse.

29

Yet all those sights, and all that else I saw,
  Might not my steps withhold, but that forthright
  Unto that purposd place I did me draw,
  Where as my love was lodged day and night: 1975
  The temple of great *Venus*, that is hight
  The Queene of beautie, and of love the mother,
  There worshipped of every living wight;
  Whose goodly workmanship farre past all other
That ever were on earth, all were they set together.   1980

30

Not that same famous Temple of *Diane*,
  Whose hight all *Ephesus* did oversee,
  And which all *Asia* sought with vowes prophane,
  One of the worlds seven wonders sayd to bee,
  Might match with this by many a degree: 1985
  Nor that, which that wise King of *Iurie* framed,
  With endlesse cost, to be th'Almighties see;
  Nor all that else through all the world is named
To all the heathen Gods, might like to this be clamed.

31

I much admyring that so goodly frame,   1990
   Unto the porch approcht, which open stood;
   But therein sate an amiable Dame,
   That seem'd to be of very sober mood,
   And in her semblant shewed great womanhood:
   Strange was her tyre; for on her head a crowne   1995
   She wore much like unto a Danisk hood,
   Poudred with pearle and stone, and all her gowne
Enwoven was with gold, that raught full low a downe.

32

On either side of her, two young men stood,
   Both strongly arm'd, as fearing one another;   2000
   Yet were they brethren both of halfe the blood,
   Begotten by two fathers of one mother,
   Though of contrarie natures each to other:
   The one of them hight *Love*, the other *Hate*,
   Hate was the elder, *Love* the younger brother;   2005
   Yet was the younger stronger in his state
Then th'elder, and him maystred still in all debate.

33

Nathlesse that Dame so well them tempred both,
   That she them forced hand to ioyne in hand,
   Albe that *Hatred* was thereto full loth,   2010
   And turn'd his face away, as he did stand,
   Unwilling to behold that lovely band.
   Yet she was of such grace and vertuous might,
   That her commaundment he could not withstand,
   But bit his lip for felonous despight,   2015
And gnasht his yron tuskes at that displeasing sight.

34

Concord she cleeped in common reed,
 Mother of blessed *Peace*, and *Friendship* trew;
 They both her twins, both borne of heavenly seed,
 And she her selfe likewise divinely grew;   2020
 The which right well her workes divine did shew:
 For strength, and wealth, and happinesse she lends,
 And strife, and warre, and anger does subdew:
 Of litle much, of foes she maketh frends,
And to afflicted minds sweet rest and quiet sends. 2025

35

By her the heaven is in his course contained,
 And all the world in state unmoved stands,
 As their Almightie maker first ordained,
 And bound them with inviolable bands;
 Else would the waters overflow the lands,   2030
 And fire devoure the ayre, and hell them quight,
 But that she holds them with her blessed hands.
 She is the nourse of pleasure and delight,
And unto *Venus* grace the gate doth open right.

36

By her I entring halfe dismayed was,   2035
 But she in gentle wise me entertayned,
 And twixt her selfe and *Love* did let me pas;
 But *Hatred* would my entrance have restrayned,
 And with his club me threatned to have brayned,
 Had not the Ladie with her powrefull speach 2040
 Him from his wicked will uneath refrayned;
 And th'other eke his malice did empeach,
Till I was throughly past the perill of his reach.

37

Into the inmost Temple thus I came,
  Which fuming all with frankensence I found,   2045
  And odours rising from the altars flame,
  Upon an hundred marble pillors round
  The roofe up high was reared from the ground,
  All deckt with crownes, and chaynes, and girlands gay,
  And thousand pretious gifts worth many a pound,   2050
  The which sad lovers for their vowes did pay;
And all the ground was strow'd with flowres, as fresh as
    May.

38

An hundred Altars round about were set,
  All flaming with their sacrifices fire,
  That with the steme thereof the Temple swet,   2055
  Which rould in clouds to heaven did aspire,
  And in them bore true lovers vowes entire:
  And eke an hundred brasen caudrons bright,
  To bath in ioy and amorous desire,
  Every of which was to a damzell hight;   2060
For all the Priests were damzels, in soft linnen dight.

39

Right in the midst the Goddesse selfe did stand
  Upon an altar of some costly masse,
  Whose substance was uneath to understand:
  For neither pretious stone, nor durefull brasse,   2065
  Nor shining gold, nor mouldring clay it was;
  But much more rare and pretious to esteeme,
  Pure in aspect, and like to christall glasse,
  Yet glasse was not, if one did rightly deeme,
But being faire and brickle, likest glasse did seeme.   2070

40

But it in shape and beautie did excell
  All other Idoles, which the heathen adore,
  Farre passing that, which by surpassing skill
  Phidias did make in *Paphos* Isle of yore,
  With which that wretched Greeke, that life forlore,   2075
  Did fall in love: yet this much fairer shined,
  But covered with a slender veile afore;
  And both her feete and legs together twyned
Were with a snake, whose head and tail were fast
    combyned.

41

The cause why she was covered with a vele,   2080
  Was hard to know, for that her Priests the same
  From peoples knowledge labour'd to concele.
  But sooth it was not sure for womanish shame,
  Nor any blemish, which the worke mote blame;
  But for, they say, she hath both kinds in one,   2085
  Both male and female, both under one name:
  She syre and mother is her selfe alone,
Begets and eke conceives, ne needeth other none.

42

And all about her necke and shoulders flew
  A flocke of litle loves, and sports, and ioyes,   2090
  With nimble wings of gold and purple hew;
  Whose shapes seem'd not like to terrestriall boyes,
  But like to Angels playing heavenly toyes;
  The whilest their eldest brother was away,
  Cupid their eldest brother; he enioyes   2095
  The wide kingdome of love with Lordly sway,
And to his law compels all creatures to obay.

43

And all about her altar scattered lay
  Great sorts of lovers piteously complayning,
  Some of their losse, some of their loves delay,   2100
  Some of their pride, some paragons disdayning,
  Some fearing fraud, some fraudulently fayning,
  As every one had cause of good or ill.
  Amongst the rest some one through loves constrayning,
  Tormented sore, could not containe it still,   2105
But thus brake forth, that all the temple it did fill.

44

Great *Venus*, Queene of beautie and of grace,
  The ioy of Gods and men, that under skie
  Doest fayrest shine, and most adorne thy place,
  That with thy smyling looke doest pacifie   2110
  The raging seas, and makst the stormes to flie;
  Thee goddesse, thee the winds, the clouds doe feare,
  And when thou spredst thy mantle forth on hie,
  The waters play and pleasant lands appeare,
And heavens laugh, and al the world shews ioyous cheare. 2115

45

Then doth the dædale earth throw forth to thee
  Out of her fruitfull lap aboundant flowres,
  And then all living wights, soone as they see
  The spring breake forth out of his lusty bowres,
  They all doe learne to play the Paramours;   2120
  First doe the merry birds, thy pretty pages
  Privily pricked with thy lustfull powres,
  Chirpe loud to thee out of their leavy cages,
And thee their mother call to coole their kindly rages.

46

Then doe the salvage beasts begin to play   2125
   Their pleasant friskes, and loath their wonted food;
   The Lyons rore, the Tygres loudly bray,
   The raging Buls rebellow through the wood,
   And breaking forth, dare tempt the deepest flood,
   To come where thou doest draw them with desire: 2130
   So all things else, that nourish vitall blood,
   Soone as with fury thou doest them inspire,
In generation seeke to quench their inward fire.

47

So all the world by thee at first was made,
   And dayly yet thou doest the same repayre: 2135
   Ne ought on earth that merry is and glad,
   Ne ought on earth that lovely is and fayre,
   But thou the same for pleasure didst prepayre.
   Thou art the root of all that ioyous is,
   Great God of men and women, queene of th'ayre,   2140
   Mother of laughter, and welspring of blisse,
O graunt that of my love at last I may not misse.

48

So did he say: but I with murmure soft,
   That none might heare the sorrow of my hart,
   Yet inly groning deepe and sighing oft,   2145
   Besought her to graunt ease unto my smart,
   And to my wound her gratious help impart.
   Whilest thus I spake, behold with happy eye
   I spyde, where at the Idoles feet apart
   A bevie of fayre damzels close did lye,   2150
   Wayting when as the Antheme should be sung on hye.

49

The first of them did seeme of ryper yeares,
    And graver countenance then all the rest;
    Yet all the rest were eke her equall peares,
    Yet unto her obayed all the best.   2155
    Her name was *Womanhood*, that she exprest
    By her sad semblant and demeanure wyse:
    For stedfast still her eyes did fixed rest,
    Ne rov'd at randon after gazers guyse,
Whose luring baytes oftimes doe heedlesse harts entyse. 2160

50

And next to her sate goodly *Shamefastnesse*,
    Ne ever durst her eyes from ground upreare,
    Ne ever once did looke up from her desse,
    As if some blame of evill she did feare,
    That in her cheekes made roses oft appeare.   2165
    And her against sweet *Cherefulnesse* was placed,
    Whose eyes like twinkling stars in evening cleare,
    Were deckt with smyles, that all sad humors chaced,
And darted forth delights, the which her goodly graced.

51

And next to her sate sober *Modestie*,   2170
    Holding her hand upon her gentle hart;
    And her against sate comely *Curtesie*,
    That unto every person knew her part;
    And her before was seated overthwart
    Soft *Silence*, and submisse *Obedience*,   2175
    Both linckt together never to dispart,
    Both gifts of God not gotten but from thence,
Both girlonds of his Saints against their foes offence.

52

Thus sate they all a round in seemely rate:
   And in the midst of them a goodly mayd,   2180
   Even in the lap of *Womanhood* there sate,
   The which was all in lilly white arayd,
   With silver streames amongst the linnen stray'd;
   Like to the Morne, when first her shyning face
   Hath to the gloomy world it selfe bewray'd,   2185
   That same was fayrest *Amoret* in place,
Shyning with beauties light, and heavenly vertues grace.

V. vii. 1–23

1

Nought is on earth more sacred or divine,
   That Gods and men doe equally adore,
   Then this same vertue, that doth right define: 2190
   For the'hevens themselves, whence mortal men implore
   Right in their wrongs, are rul'd by righteous lore
   Of highest Iove, who doth true iustice deale
   To his inferiour Gods, and evermore
   Therewith containes his heavenly Commonweale: 2195
The skill whereof to Princes hearts he doth reveale.

2

Well therefore did the antique world invent,
   That Iustice was a God of soveraine grace,
   And altars unto him, and temples lent,
   And heavenly honours in the highest place;   2200
   Calling him great *Osyris*, of the race
   Of th'old Ægyptian Kings, that whylome were;
   With fayned colours shading a true case:
   For that *Osyris*, whilest he lived here,
The iustest man alive, and truest did appeare.   2205

Ks

3

His wife was *Isis*, whom they likewise made
  A Goddesse of great powre and soverainty,
  And in her person cunningly did shade
  That part of Iustice, which is Equity,
  Whereof I have to treat here presently.   2210
  Unto whose temple when as *Britomart*
  Arrived, shee with great humility
  Did enter in, ne would that night depart;
But *Talus* mote not be admitted to her part.

4

There she received was in goodly wize   2215
  Of many Priests, which duely did attend
  Uppon the rites and daily sacrifize,
  All clad in linnen robes with silver hemd;
  And on their heads with long locks comely kemd,
  They wore rich Mitres shaped like the Moone,   2220
  To shew that *Isis* doth the Moone portend;
  Like as *Osyris* signifies the Sunne.
For that they both like race in equall iustice runne.

5

The Championesse them greeting, as she could,
  Was thence by them into the Temple led;   2225
  Whose goodly building when she did behould,
  Borne uppon stately pillours, all dispred
  With shining gold, and arched over hed,
  She wondred at the workemans passing skill,
  Whose like before she never saw nor red;   2230
  And thereuppon long while stood gazing still,
But thought, that she thereon could never gaze her fill.

6

Thence forth unto the Idoll they her brought,
  The which was framed all of silver fine,
  So well as could with cunning hand be wrought,   2235
  And clothed all in garments made of line,
  Hemd all about with fringe of silver twine.
  Uppon her head she wore a Crowne of gold,
  To shew that she had powre in things divine;
  And at her feete a Crocodile was rold,   2240
That with his wreathed taile her middle did enfold.

7

One foote was set uppon the Crocodile,
  And on the ground the other fast did stand,
  So meaning to suppresse both forged guile,
  And open force: and in her other hand   2245
  She stretched forth a long white sclender wand.
  Such was the Goddesse; whom when *Britomart*
  Had long beheld, her selfe uppon the land
  She did prostrate, and with right humble hart,
Unto her selfe her silent prayers did impart.   2250

8

To which the Idoll as it were inclining,
  Her wand did move with amiable looke,
  By outward shew her inward sence desining.
  Who well perceiving, how her wand she shooke,
  It as a token of good fortune tooke.   2255
  By this the day with dampe was overcast,
  And ioyous light the house of *Iove* forsooke:
  Which when she saw, her helmet she unlaste,
And by the altars side her selfe to slumber plaste.

9

For other beds the Priests there used none,   2260
  But on their mother Earths deare lap did lie,
  And bake their sides uppon the cold hard stone,
  T'enure them selves to sufferaunce thereby
  And proud rebellious flesh to mortify.
  For by the vow of their religion   2265
  They tied were to stedfast chastity,
  And continence of life, that all forgon,
They mote the better tend to their devotion.

10

Therefore they mote not taste of fleshly food,
  Ne feed on ought, the which doth bloud containe,   2270
  Ne drinke of wine, for wine they say is blood,
  Even the bloud of Gyants, which were slaine,
  By thundring Iove in the Phlegrean plaine:
  For which the earth (as they the story tell)
  Wroth with the Gods, which to perpetuall paine   2275
  Had damn'd her sonnes, which gainst them did rebell,
With inward griefe and malice did against them swell.

11

And of their vitall bloud, the which was shed
  Into her pregnant bosome, forth she brought
  The fruitfull vine, whose liquor blouddy red   2280
  Having the mindes of men with fury fraught,
  Mote in them stirre up old rebellious thought,
  To make new warre against the Gods againe:
  Such is the powre of that same fruit, that nought
  The fell contagion may thereof restraine,   2285
Ne within reasons rule, her madding mood containe.

12

There did the warlike Maide her selfe repose,
    Under the wings of *Isis* all that night,
    And with sweete rest her heavy eyes did close,
    After that long daies toile and weary plight.   2290
    Where whilest her earthly parts with soft delight
    Of sencelesse sleepe did deeply drowned lie,
    There did appeare unto her heavenly spright
    A wondrous vision, which did close implie
The course of all her fortune and posteritie.   2295

13

Her seem'd, as she was doing sacrifize
    To *Isis*, deckt with Mitre on her hed,
    And linnen stole after those Priests guize,
    All sodainely she saw transfigured
    Her linnen stole to robe of scarlet red,   2300
    And Moone-like Mitre to a Crowne of gold,
    That even she her selfe much wondered
    At such a chaunge, and ioyed to behold
Her selfe, adorn'd with gems and iewels manifold.

14

And in the midst of her felicity,   2305
    An hideous tempest seemed from below,
    To rise through all the Temple sodainely,
    That from the Altar all about did blow
    The holy fire, and all the embers strow
    Uppon the ground, which kindled privily,   2310
    Into outragious flames unwares did grow,
    That all the Temple put in ieopardy
Of flaming, and her selfe in great perplexity.

15

With that the Crocodile, which sleeping lay
   Under the Idols feete in fearelesse bowre,   2315
   Seem'd to awake in horrible dismay,
   As being troubled with that stormy stowre;
   And gaping greedy wide, did streight devoure
   Both flames and tempest: with which growen great,
   And swolne with pride of his owne peerelesse powre, 2320
   He gan to threaten her likewise to eat;
But that the Goddesse with her rod him backe did beat.

16

Tho turning all his pride to humblesse meeke,
   Him selfe before her feete he lowly threw,
   And gan for grace and love of her to seeke: 2325
   Which she accepting, he so neare her drew,
   That of his game she soone enwombed grew,
   And forth did bring a Lion of great might;
   That shortly did all other beasts subdew.
   With that she waked, full of fearefull fright,   2330
And doubtfully dismayd through that so uncouth sight.

17

So thereuppon long while she musing lay,
   With thousand thoughts feeding her fantasie,
   Untill she spide the lampe of lightsome day,
   Up-lifted in the porch of heaven hie.   2335
   Then up she rose fraught with melancholy,
   And forth into the lower parts did pas;
   Whereas the Priestes she found full busily
   About their holy things for morrow Mas:
Whom she saluting faire, faire resaluted was.   2340

18

But by the change of her unchearefull looke,
   They might perceive, she was not well in plight;
   Or that some pensivenesse to heart she tooke.
   Therefore thus one of them, who seem'd in sight
   To be the greatest, and the gravest wight,   2345
   To her bespake; Sir Knight it seemes to me,
   That thorough evill rest of this last night,
   Or ill apayd; or much dismayd ye be,
That by your change of cheare is easie for to see.

19

Certes (sayd she) sith ye so well have spide   2350
   The troublous passion of my pensive mind,
   I will not seeke the same from you to hide,
   But will my cares unfolde, in hope to find
   Your aide, to guide me out of errour blind.
   Say on (quoth he) the secret of your hart: 2355
   For by the holy vow, which me doth bind,
   I am adiur'd, best counsell to impart
To all, that shall require my comfort in their smart.

20

Then gan she to declare the whole discourse
   Of all that vision, which to her appeard,   2360
   As well as to her minde it had recourse.
   All which when he unto the end had heard,
   Like to a weake faint-hearted man he fared,
   Through great astonishment of that strange sight;
   And with long locks up-standing, stifly stared   2365
   Like one adawed with some dreadfull spright.
So fild with heavenly fury, thus he her behight.

21

Magnificke Virgin, that in queint disguise
  Of British armes doest maske thy royall blood,
  So to pursue a perillous emprize,   2370
  How couldst thou weene, through that disguized hood,
  To hide thy state from being understood?
  Can from th'immortall Gods ought hidden bee?
  They doe thy linage, and thy Lordly brood;
  They doe thy sire, lamenting sore for thee;   2375
  They doe thy love, forlorne in womens thraldome see.

22

The end whereof, and all the long event,
  They doe to thee in this same dreame discover.
  For that same Crocodile doth represent
  The righteous Knight, that is thy faithfull lover,   2380
  Like to *Osyris* in all iust endever.
  For that same Crocodile *Osyris* is,
  That under *Isis* feete doth sleepe for ever:
  To shew that clemence oft in things amis,
Restraines those sterne behests, and cruell doomes of his. 2385

23

That Knight shall all the troublous stormes asswage,
  And raging flames, that many foes shall reare,
  To hinder thee from the iust heritage
  Of thy sires Crowne, and from thy countrey deare.
  Then shalt thou take him to thy loved fere,   2390
  And ioyne in equall portion of thy realme.
  And afterwards a sonne to him shalt beare,
  That Lion-like shall shew his powre extreame.
So blesse thee God, and give thee ioyance of thy dreame.

V. ix. 27–50

27

They passing by, were guyded by degree   2395
  Unto the presence of that gratious Queene:
  Who sate on high, that she might all men see,
  And might of all men royally be seene,
  Upon a throne of gold full bright and sheene,
  Adorned all with gemmes of endlesse price,   2400
  As either might for wealth have gotten bene,
  Or could be fram'd by workmans rare device;
And all embost with Lyons and with Flour-delice.

28

All over her a cloth of state was spred,
  Not of rich tissew, nor of cloth of gold,   2405
  Nor of ought else, that may be richest red,
  But like a cloud, as likest may be told,
  That her brode spreading wings did wyde unfold;
  Whose skirts were bordred with bright sunny beams,
  Glistring like gold, amongst the plights enrold,   2410
  And here and there shooting forth silver streames,
Mongst which crept litle Angels through the glittering
  gleames.

29

Seemed those litle Angels did uphold
  The cloth of state, and on their purpled wings
  Did beare the pendants, through their nimblesse bold: 2415
  Besides a thousand more of such, as sings
  Hymnes to high God, and carols heavenly things,
  Encompassed the throne, on which she sate:
  She Angel-like, the heyre of ancient kings
  And mightie Conquerors, in royall state,   2420
Whylest kings and kesars at her feet did them prostrate.

30

Thus she did sit in soverayne Maiestie,
  Holding a Scepter in her royall hand,
  The sacred pledge of peace and clemencie,
  With which high God had blest her happie land,   2425
  Maugre so many foes, which did withstand.
  But at her feet her sword was likewise layde,
  Whose long rest rusted the bright steely brand;
  Yet when as foes enforst, or friends sought ayde,
She could it sternely draw, that all the world dismayde. 2430

31

And round about, before her feet there sate
  A bevie of faire Virgins clad in white,
  That goodly seem'd t'adorne her royall state,
  All lovely daughters of high *Iove*, that hight
  Litæ, by him begot in loves delight,   2435
  Upon the righteous *Themis*: those they say
  Upon *Ioves* iudgement seat wayt day and night,
  And when in wrath he threats the worlds decay,
They doe his anger calme, and cruell vengeance stay.

32

They also doe by his divine permission   2440
  Upon the thrones of mortall Princes tend,
  And often treat for pardon and remission
  To suppliants, through frayltie which offend.
  Those did upon *Mercillaes* throne attend:
  Iust *Dice*, wise *Eunomie*, myld *Eirene*,   2445
  And them amongst, her glorie to commend,
  Sate goodly *Temperance* in garments clene,
And sacred *Reverence*, yborne of heavenly strene.

33

Thus did she sit in royall rich estate,
  Admyr'd of many, honoured of all,   2450
   Whylest underneath her feete, thereas she sate,
   An huge great Lyon lay, that mote appall
   An hardie courage, like captived thrall,
   With a strong yron chaine and coller bound,
   That once he could not move, nor quich at all;   2455
   Yet did he murmure with rebellious sound,
And softly royne, when salvage choler gan redound.

34

So sitting high in dreaded soverayntie,
  Those two strange knights were to her presence brought:
   Who bowing low before her Maiestie,   2460
   Did to her myld obeysance, as they ought,
   And meekest boone, that they imagine mought.
   To whom she eke inclyning her withall,
   As a faire stoupe of her high soaring thought,
   A chearefull countenance on them let fall,   2465
Yet tempred with some maiestie imperiall.

35

As the bright sunne, what time his fierie teme
  Towards the westerne brim begins to draw,
  Gins to abate the brightnesse of his beme,
  And fervour of his flames somewhat adaw: 2470
  So did this mightie Ladie, when she saw
  Those two strange knights such homage to her make,
  Bate somewhat of that Maiestie and awe,
  That whylome wont to doe so many quake,
And with more myld aspect those two to entertake.   2475

36

Now at that instant, as occasion fell,
  When these two stranger knights arriv'd in place,
  She was about affaires of common wele,
  Dealing of Iustice with indifferent grace,
  And hearing pleas of people meane and base.   2480
  Mongst which as then, there was for to be heard
  The tryall of a great and weightie case,
  Which on both sides was then debating hard:
But at the sight of these, those were a while debard.

37

But after all her princely entertayne,   2485
  To th'hearing of that former cause in hand,
  Her selfe eftsoones she gan convert againe;
  Which that those knights likewise mote understand,
  And witnesse forth aright in forrain land,
  Taking them up unto her stately throne,   2490
  Where they mote heare the matter throughly scand
  On either part, she placed th'one on th'one,
The other on the other side, and neare them none.

38

Then was there brought, as prisoner to the barre,
  A Ladie of great countenance and place,   2495
  But that she it with foule abuse did marre;
  Yet did appeare rare beautie in her face,
  But blotted with condition vile and base,
  That all her other honour did obscure,
  And titles of nobilitie deface: 2500
  Yet in that wretched semblant, she did sure
The peoples great compassion unto her allure.

39

Then up arose a person of deepe reach,
    And rare in sight, hard matters to revele;
    That well could charme his tongue, and time his speach   2505
    To all assayes; his name was called *Zele*:
    He gan that Ladie strongly to appele
    Of many haynous crymes, by her enured,
    And with sharpe reasons rang her such a pele,
    That those, whom she to pitie had allured,   2510
He now t'abhorre and loath her person had procured.

40

First gan he tell, how this that seem'd so fare
    And royally arayd, *Duessa* hight
    That false *Duessa*, which had wrought great care,
    And mickle mischiefe unto many a knight,   2515
    By her begyled, and confounded quight:
    But not for those she now in question came,
    Though also those mote question'd be aright,
    But for vyld treasons, and outrageous shame,
Which she against the dred *Mercilla* oft did frame.   2520

41

For she whylome (as ye mote yet right well
    Remember) had her counsels false conspyred,
    With faithlesse *Blandamour* and *Paridell*,
    (Both two her paramours, both by her hyred,
    And both with hope of shadowes vaine inspyred,)   2525
    And with them practiz'd, how for to depryve
    Mercilla of her crowne, by her aspyred,
    That she might it unto her selfe deryve,
And tryumph in their blood, whom she to death did dryve.

42

But through high heavens grace, which favour not   2530
  The wicked driftes of trayterous desynes,
  Gainst loiall Princes, all this cursed plot,
  Ere proofe it tooke, discovered was betymes,
  And th'actours won the meede meet for their crymes.
  Such be the meede of all, that by such mene   2535
  Unto the type of kingdomes title clymes.
  But false *Duessa* now untitled Queene,
Was brought to her sad doome, as here was to be seene.

43

Strongly did *Zele* her haynous fact enforce,
  And many other crimes of foule defame   2540
  Against her brought, to banish all remorse,
  And aggravate the horror of her blame.
  And with him to make part against her, came
  Many grave persons, that against her pled;
  First was a sage old Syre, that had to name   2545
  The *Kingdomes care*, with a white silver hed,
That many high regards and reasons gainst her red.

44

Then gan *Authority* her to appose
  With peremptorie powre, that made all mute;
  And then the law of *Nations* gainst her rose,   2550
  And reasons brought, that no man could refute;
  Next gan *Religion* gainst her to impute
  High Gods beheast, and powre of holy lawes;
  Then gan the Peoples cry and Commons sute,
  Importune care of their owne publicke cause;   2555
And lastly *Iustice* charged her with breach of lawes.

45

But then for her, on the contrarie part,
   Rose many advocates for her to plead:
   First there came *Pittie*, with full tender hart,
   And with her ioyn'd *Regard* of womanhead;   2560
   And then came *Daunger* threatning hidden dread,
   And high alliance unto forren powre;
   Then came *Nobilitie* of birth, that bread
   Great ruth through her misfortunes tragicke stowre;
And lastly *Griefe* did plead, and many teares forth powre. 2565

46

With the neare touch whereof in tender hart
   The Briton Prince was sore empassionate,
   And woxe inclined much unto her part,
   Through the sad terror of so dreadfull fate,
   And wretched ruine of so high estate,   2570
   That for great ruth his courage gan relent.
   Which when as *Zele* perceived to abate,
   He gan his earnest fervour to augment,
And many fearefull obiects to them to present.

47

He gan t'efforce the evidence anew,   2575
   And new accusements to produce in place:
   He brought forth that old hag of hellish hew,
   The cursed *Ate*, brought her face to face,
   Who privie was, and partie in the case:
   She, glad of spoyle and ruinous decay,   2580
   Did her appeach, and to her more disgrace,
   The plot of all her practise did display,
And all her traynes, and all her treasons forth did lay.

48

Then brought he forth, with griesly grim aspect,
    Abhorred *Murder*, who with bloudie knyfe   2585
    Yet dropping fresh in hand did her detect,
    And there with guiltie bloudshed charged ryfe:
    Then brought he forth *Sedition*, breeding stryfe
    In troublous wits, and mutinous uprore:
    Then brought he forth *Incontinence* of lyfe,   2590
    Even foule *Adulterie* her face before,
And lewd *Impietie*, that her accused sore.

49

All which when as the Prince had heard and seene,
    His former fancies ruth he gan repent,
    And from her partie eftsoones was drawen cleene.   2595
    But *Artegall* with constant firme intent,
    For zeale of Iustice was against her bent.
    So was she guiltie deemed of them all.
    Then *Zele* began to urge her punishment.
    And to their Queene for iudgement loudly call,   2600
Unto *Mercilla* myld for Iustice gainst the thrall.

50

But she, whose Princely breast was touched nere
    With piteous ruth of her so wretched plight,
    Though plaine she saw by all, that she did heare,
    That she of death was guiltie found by right,   2605
    Yet would not let iust vengeance on her light;
    But rather let in stead thereof to fall
    Few perling drops from her faire lampes of light;
    The which she covering with her purple pall
Would have the passion hid, and up arose withall.   2610

VI. x. 10–28

10

Unto this place when as the Elfin Knight
   Approcht, him seemed that the merry sound
   Of a shrill pipe he playing heard on hight,
   And many feete fast thumping th'hollow ground,
   That through the woods their Eccho did rebound.   2615
   He nigher drew, to weete what mote it be;
   There he a troupe of Ladies dauncing found
   Full merrily, and making gladfull glee,
And in the midst a Shepheard piping he did see.

11

He durst not enter into th'open greene,   2620
   For dread of them unwares to be descryde,
   For breaking of their daunce, if he were seene;
   But in the covert of the wood did byde,
   Beholding all, yet of them unespyde.
   There he did see, that pleased much his sight,   2625
   That even he himselfe his eyes envyde,
   An hundred naked maidens lilly white,
All raunged in a ring, and dauncing in delight.

12

All they without were raunged in a ring,
   And daunced round; but in the midst of them   2630
   Three other Ladies did both daunce and sing,
   The whilest the rest them round about did hemme,
   And like a girlond did in compasse stemme
   And in the middest of those same three, was placed
   Another Damzell, as a precious gemme,   2635
   Amidst a ring most richly well enchaced,
That with her goodly presence all the rest much graced.

Ls

13

Looke how the Crowne, which *Ariadne* wore
   Upon her yvory forehead that same day,
   That *Theseus* her unto his bridale bore,   2640
   When the bold *Centaures* made that bloudy fray,
   With the fierce *Lapithes*, which did them dismay;
   Being now placed in the firmament,
   Through the bright heaven doth her beams display,
   And is unto the starres an ornament,   2645
Which round about her move in order excellent.

14

Such was the beauty of this goodly band,
   Whose sundry parts were here too long to tell:
   But she that in the midst of them did stand,
   Seem'd all the rest in beauty to excell,   2650
   Crownd with a rosie girlond, that right well
   Did her beseeme. And ever, as the crew
   About her daunst, sweet flowres, that far did smell,
   And fragrant odours they uppon her threw;
But most of all, those three did her with gifts endew.   2655

15

Those were the Graces, daughters of delight,
   Handmaides of *Venus*, which are wont to haunt
   Uppon this hill, and daunce there day and night:
   Those three to men all gifts of grace do graunt,
   And all, that *Venus* in her selfe doth vaunt,   2660
   Is borrowed of them.   But that faire one,
   That in the midst was placed paravaunt,
   Was she to whom that shepheard pypt alone,
That made him pipe so merrily, as never none.

16

She was to weete that iolly Shepheards lasse,   2665
    Which piped there vnto that merry rout,
    That iolly shepheard, which there piped, was
    Poore *Colin Clout* (who knowes not *Colin Clout*?)
    He pypt apace, whilest they him daunst about.
    Pype iolly shepheard, pype thou now apace   2670
    Vnto thy love, that made thee low to lout:
    Thy love is present there with thee in place,
Thy love is there aduaunst to be another Grace.

17

Much wondred *Calidore* at this straunge sight,
    Whose like before his eye had neuer seene,   2675
    And standing long astonished in spright,
    And rapt with pleasaunce, wist not what to weene;
    Whether it were the traine of beauties Queene,
    Or Nymphes, or Faeries, or enchaunted show,
    With which his eyes mote haue deluded beene.   2680
    Therefore resoluing, what it was, to know,
Out of the wood he rose, and toward them did go.

18

But soone as he appeared to their vew,
    They vanisht all away out of his sight,
    And cleane were gone, which way he neuer knew;   2685
    All saue the shepheard, who for fell despight
    Of that displeasure, broke his bag-pipe quight,
    And made great mone for that vnhappy turne.
    But *Calidore*, though no lesse sory wight,
    For that mishap, yet seeing him to mourne,   2690
Drew neare, that he the truth of all by him mote learne.

19

And first him greeting, thus unto him spake,
  Haile iolly shepheard, which thy ioyous dayes
  Here leadest in this goodly merry make,
  Frequented of these gentle Nymphes alwayes,   2695
  Which to thee flocke, to heare thy lovely layes;
  Tell me, what mote these dainty Damzels be,
  Which here with thee doe make their pleasant playes?
  Right happy thou, that mayst them freely see:
But why when I them saw, fled they away from me?   2700

20

Not I so happy, answerd then that swaine,
  As thou unhappy, which them thence didst chace,
  Whome by no meanes thou canst recall againe,
  For being gone, none can them bring in place,
  But whom they of themselves list so to grace.   2705
  Right sory I, (saide then Sir *Calidore*,)
  That my ill fortune did them hence displace.
  But since things passed none may now restore,
Tell me, what were they all, whose lacke thee grieves
    so sore.

21

Tho gan that shepheard thus for to dilate;   2710
  Then wote thou shepheard, whatsoever thou bee,
  That all those Ladies, which thou sawest late,
  Are *Venus* Damzels, all within her fee,
  But differing in honour and degree:
  They all are Graces, which on her depend,   2715
  Besides a thousand more, which ready bee
  Her to adorne, when so she forth doth wend:
But those three in the midst, doe chiefe on her attend.

22

They are the daughters of sky-ruling Iove,
   By him begot of faire *Eurynome*,   2720
   The Oceans daughter, in this pleasant grove,
   As he this way comming from feastfull glee,
   Of *Thetis* wedding with *Æacidee*,
   In sommers shade him selfe here rested weary.
   The first of them hight mylde *Euphrosyne*,   2725
   Next faire *Aglaia*, last *Thalia* merry:
Sweete Goddesses all three which me in mirth do cherry.

23

These three on men all gracious gifts bestow,
   Which decke the body or adorne the mynde,
   To make them lovely or well favoured show,   2730
   As comely carriage, entertainement kynde,
   Sweete semblaunt, friendly offices that bynde,
   And all the complements of curtesie:
   They teach us, how to each degree and kynde
   We should our selves demeane, to low, to hie;   2735
To friends, to foes, which skill men call Civility.

24

Therefore they alwaies smoothly seeme to smile,
   That we likewise should mylde and gentle be,
   And also naked are, that without guile
   Or false dissemblaunce all them plaine may see,   2740
   Simple and true from covert malice free:
   And eeke them selves so in their daunce they bore,
   That two of them still froward seem'd to bee,
   But one still towards shew'd her selfe afore;
That good should from us goe, then come in greater store.   2745

25

Such were those Goddesses, which ye did see;
    But that fourth Mayd, which there amidst them traced,
    Who can aread, what creature mote she bee,
    Whether a creature, or a goddesse graced
    With heavenly gifts from heven first enraced?   2750
    But what so sure she was, she worthy was,
    To be the fourth with those three other placed:
    Yet was she certes but a countrey lasse,
Yet she all other countrey lasses farre did passe.

26

So farre as doth the daughter of the day,   2755
    All other lesser lights in light excell,
    So farre doth she in beautyfull array,
    Above all other lasses beare the bell,
    Ne lesse in vertue that beseemes her well,
    Doth she exceede the rest of all her race,   2760
    For which the Graces that here wont to dwell,
    Have for more honor brought her to this place,
And graced her so much to be another Grace.

27

Another Grace she well deserves to be,
    In whom so many Graces gathered are,   2765
    Excelling much the meane of her degree;
    Divine resemblaunce, beauty soveraine rare,
    Firme Chastity, that spight ne blemish dare;
    All which she with such courtesie doth grace,
    That all her peres cannot with her compare,   2770
    But quite are dimmed, when she is in place.
She made me often pipe and now to pipe apace.

28

Sunne of the world, great glory of the sky,
   That all the earth doest lighten with thy rayes,
   Great *Gloriana*, greatest Maiesty,   2775
   Pardon thy shepheard, mongst so many layes,
   As he hath sung of thee in all his dayes,
   To make one minime of thy poore handmayd,
   And underneath thy feete to place her prayse,
   That when thy glory shall be farre displayd   2780
To future age of her this mention may be made.

VII. vii. 3–27, 47–59

3

Now, at the time that was before agreed,
   The Gods assembled all on *Arlo* hill;
   As well those that are sprung of heavenly seed,
   As those that all the other world doe fill,   2785
   And rule both sea and land unto their will:
   Onely th'infernall Powers might not appeare;
   As well for horror of their count'naunce ill,
   As for th'unruly fiends which they did feare;
Yet *Pluto* and *Proserpina* were present there.   2790

4

And thither also came all other creatures,
   What-ever life or motion doe retaine,
   According to their sundry kinds of features;
   That *Arlo* scarsly could them all containe;
   So full they filled every hill and Plaine: 2795
   And had not *Natures* Sergeant (that is *Order*)
   Them well disposed by his busie paine,
   And raunged farre abroad in every border,
They would have caused much confusion and disorder.

5

Then forth issewed (great goddesse) great dame *Nature*   2800
   With goodly port and gracious Maiesty;
   Being far greater and more tall of stature
   Then any of the gods or Powers on hie:
   Yet certes by her face and physnomy,
   Whether she man or woman inly were,   2805
   That could not any creature well descry:
   For, with a veile that wimpled every where
Her head and face was hid, that mote to none appeare.

6

That some doe say was so by skill devized,
   To hide the terror of her uncouth hew,   2810
   From mortall eyes that should be sore agrized;
   For that her face did like a Lion shew,
   That eye of wight could not indure to view:
   But others tell that it so beautious was,
   And round about such beames of splendor threw,   2815
   That it the Sunne a thousand times did pass,
Ne could be seene, but like an image in a glass.

7

That well may seemen true: for, well I weene
   That this same day, when she on *Arlo* sat,
   Her garment was so bright and wondrous sheene,   2820
   That my fraile wit cannot devize to what
   It to compare, nor finde like stuffe to that,
   As those three sacred *Saints*, though else most wise,
   Yet on mount *Thabor* quite their wits forgat,
   When they their glorious Lord in strange disguise   2825
Transfigur'd sawe; his garments so did daze their eyes.

8

In a fayre Plaine upon an equall Hill,
   She placed was in a pavilion;
   Not such as Craftes-men by their idle skill
   Are wont for Princes states to fashion: 2830
   But th'earth her self of her owne motion,
   Out of her fruitfull bosome made to growe
   Most dainty trees; that, shooting up anon,
   Did seeme to bow their bloosming heads full lowe,
For homage unto her, and like a throne did shew. 2835

9

So hard it is for any living wight,
   All her array and vestiments to tell,
   That old *Dan Geffrey* (in whose gentle spright
   The pure well head of Poesie did dwell)
   In his *Foules parley* durst not with it mel, 2840
   But it transferd to *Alane*, who he thought
   Had in his *Plaint of kindes* describ'd it well:
   Which who will read set forth so as it ought,
Go seek he out that *Alane* where he may be sought.

10

And all the earth far underneath her feete 2845
   Was dight with flowres, that voluntary grew
   Out of the ground, and sent forth odours sweet;
   Tenne thousand mores of sundry sent and hew,
   That might delight the smell, or please the view;
   The which, the Nymphes, from all the brooks thereby 2850
   Had gathered, which they at her foot-stoole threw;
   That richer seem'd then any tapestry,
That Princes bowres adorne with painted imagery.

11

And *Mole* himselfe, to honour her the more,
    Did deck himself in freshest faire attire,   2855
    And his high head, that seemeth alwaies hore
    With hardned frosts of former winters ire,
    He with an Oaken girlond now did tire,
    As if the love of some new Nymph late seene,
    Had in him kindled youthfull fresh desire,   2860
    And made him change his gray attire to greene;
Ah gentle *Mole*! such ioyance hath thee well beseene.

12

Was never so great ioyance since the day,
    That all the gods whylome assembled were,
    On *Hæmus* hill in their divine array,   2865
    To celebrate the solemne bridall cheare,
    Twixt *Peleus*, and dame *Thetis* pointed there;
    Where *Phœbus* self, that god of Poets hight,
    They say did sing the spousall hymne full cleere,
    That all the gods were ravisht with delight   2870
Of his celestiall song, and Musicks wondrous might.

13

This great Granmother of all creatures bred
    Great *Nature*, ever young yet full of eld,
    Still mooving, yet unmoved from her sted;
    Unseene of any, yet of all beheld;   2875
    Thus sitting in her throne as I have teld,
    Before her came dame *Mutabilitie*;
    And being lowe before her presence feld,
    With meek obaysance and humilitie,
Thus gan her plaintif Plea, with words to amplifie;   2880

14

To thee O greatest goddesse, onely great,
 An humble suppliant loe, I lowely fly
 Seeking for Right, which I of thee entreat;
 Who Right to all dost deale indifferently,
 Damning all Wrong and tortious Iniurie,   2885
 Which any of thy creatures doe to other
 (Oppressing them with power, unequally)
 Sith of them all thou art the equall mother,
And knittest each to each, as brother unto brother.

15

To thee therefore of this same *Iove* I plaine,   2890
 And of his fellow gods that faine to be,
 That challenge to themselves the whole worlds raign;
 Of which, the greatest part is due to me,
 And heaven it selfe by heritage in Fee:
 For, heaven and earth I both alike do deeme,   2895
 Sith heaven and earth are both alike to thee;
 And, gods no more then men thou doest esteeme:
For, even the gods to thee, as men to gods do seeme.

16

Then weigh, O soveraigne goddesse, by what right
 These gods do claime the worlds whole soveraity; 2900
 And that is onely dew unto thy might
 Arrogate to themselves ambitiously:
 As for the gods owne principality,
 Which *Iove* usurpes uniustly; that to be
 My heritage, *Iove's* self cannot deny,   2905
 From my great Grandsire *Titan*, unto mee,
Deriv'd by dew descent; as is well knowen to thee.

17

Yet mauger *Iove*, and all his gods beside,
　　I doe possesse the worlds most regiment;
　　As, if ye please it into parts divide,　　　　　　2910
　　And every parts inholders to convent,
　　Shall to your eyes appeare incontinent.
　　And first, the Earth (great mother of us all)
　　That only seems unmov'd and permanent,
　　And unto *Mutability* not thrall;　　　　　　　　2915
Yet is she chang'd in part, and eeke in generall.

18

For, all that from her springs, and is ybredde,
　　How-ever fayre it flourish for a time,
　　Yet see we soone decay; and, being dead,
　　To turne again unto their earthly slime:　　　　2920
　　Yet, out of their decay and mortall crime,
　　We daily see new creatures to arize;
　　And of their Winter spring another Prime,
　　Unlike in forme, and chang'd by strange disguise:
So turne they still about, and change in restlesse wise.　2925

19

As for her tenants; that is, man and beasts,
　　The beasts we daily see massacred dy,
　　As thralls and vassalls unto mens beheasts:
　　And men themselves doe change continually,
　　From youth to eld, from wealth to poverty,　　2930
　　From good to bad, from bad to worst of all.
　　Ne doe their bodies only flit and fly:
　　But eeke their minds (which they immortall call)
Still change and vary thoughts, as new occasions fall.

20

Ne is the water in more constant case;   2935
    Whether those same on high, or these belowe.
    For, th'Ocean moveth stil, from place to place;
    And every River still doth ebbe and flowe:
    Ne any Lake, that seems most still and slowe;
    Ne Poole so small, that can his smoothnesse holde,   2940
    When any winde doth under heaven blowe;
    With which, the clouds are also tost and roll'd;
Now like great Hills; and, streight, like sluces, them unfold.

21

So likewise are all watry living wights
    Still tost, and turned, with continuall change,   2945
    Never abyding in their stedfast plights.
    The fish, still floting, doe at randon range,
    And never rest; but evermore exchange
    Their dwelling places, as the streames them carrie:
    Ne have the watry foules a certaine grange,   2950
    Wherein to rest, ne in one stead do tarry;
But flitting still doe flie, and still their places vary.

22

Next is the Ayre: which who feeles not by sense
    (For, of all sense it is the middle meane)
    To flit still? and, with subtill influence   2955
    Of his thin spirit, all creatures to maintaine,
    In state of life? O weake life! that does leane
    On thing so tickle as th'unsteady ayre;
    Which every howre is chang'd, and altred cleane
    With every blast that bloweth fowle or faire: 2960
The faire doth it prolong; the fowle doth it impaire.

23

Therein the changes infinite beholde,
    Which to her creatures every minute chaunce;
    Now, boyling hot: streight, friezing deadly cold:
    Now, faire sun-shine, that makes all skip and daunce: 2965
    Streight, bitter storms and balefull countenance,
    That makes them all to shiver and to shake:
    Rayne, hayle, and snowe do pay them sad penance,
    And dreadfull thunder-claps (that makes them quake)
With flames and flashing lights that thousand changes   2970
    make.

24

Last is the fire: which, though it live for ever,
    Ne can be quenched quite; yet, every day,
    Wee see his parts, so soone as they do sever,
    To lose their heat, and shortly to decay;
    So, makes himself his owne consuming pray.   2975
    Ne any living creatures doth he breed:
    But all, that are of others bredd, doth slay;
    And, with their death, his cruell life dooth feed;
Nought leaving but their barren ashes, without seede.

25

Thus, all these fower (the which the ground-work bee   2980
    Of all the world, and of all living wights)
    To thousand sorts of *Change* we subiect see.
    Yet are they chang'd (by other wondrouss lights)
    Into themselves, and lose their native mights;
    The Fire to Aire, and th'Ayre to Water sheere,   2985
    And Water into Earth: yet Water fights
    With Fire, and Aire with Earth approaching neere:
Yet all are in one body, and as one appeare.

26

So, in them all raignes *Mutabilitie*;
  How-ever these, that Gods themselves do call,   2990
  Of them doe claime the rule and soveraity:
  As, *Vesta*, of the fire æthereall;
  Vulcan, of this, with us so usuall;
  Ops, of the earth; and *Iuno* of the Ayre;
  Neptune, of Seas; and Nymphes, of Rivers all.   2995
  For, all those Rivers to me subiect are:
And all the rest, which they usurp, be all my share.

27

Which to approven true, as I have told,
  Vouchsafe, O goddesse, to thy presence call
  The rest which doe the world in being hold: 3000
  As, times and seasons of the yeare that fall:
  Of all the which, demand in generall,
  Or iudge thy selfe, by verdit of thine eye,
  Whether to me they are not subiect all.
  Nature did yeeld thereto; and by-and-by,   3005
Bade *Order* call them all, before her Maiesty. . . .

47

When these were past, thus gan the *Titanesse*;
  Lo, mighty mother, now be iudge and say,
  Whether in all thy creatures more or lesse
  CHANGE doth not raign and beare the greatest sway: 3010
  For, who sees not, that *Time* on all doth pray?
  But *Times* do change and move continually.
  So nothing here long standeth in one stay:
  Wherefore, this lower world who can deny
But to be subiect still to *Mutabilitie*?   3015

48

Then thus gan *Iove*; Right true it is, that these
  And all things else that under heaven dwell
  Are chaung'd of *Time*, who doth them all disseise
  Of being: But, who is it (to me tell)
  That *Time* himselfe doth move and still compell   3020
  To keepe his course? Is not that namely wee
  Which poure that vertue from our heavenly cell,
  That moves them all, and makes them changed be?
So them we gods doe rule, and in them also thee.

49

To whom, thus *Mutability*: The things   3025
  Which we see not how they are mov'd and swayd,
  Ye may attribute to your selves as Kings,
  And say they by your secret powre are made:
  But what we see not, who shall us perswade?
  But were they so, as ye them faine to be,   3030
  Mov'd by your might, and ordred by your ayde;
  Yet what if I can prove, that even yee.
Your selves are likewise chang'd, and subiect unto mee?

50

And first, concerning her that is the first,
  Even you faire *Cynthia*, whom so much ye make   3035
  Ioves dearest darling, she was bred and nurst
  On *Cynthus* hill, whence she her name did take:
  Then is she mortall borne, how-so ye crake;
  Besides, her face and countenance every day
  We changed see, and sundry forms partake,   3040
  Now hornd, now round, now bright, now brown and
      gray:
So that *as changefull as the Moone* men use to say.

51

Next, *Mercury*, who though he lesse appeare
   To change his hew, and alwayes seeme as one;
   Yet, he his course doth altar every yeare,   3045
   And is of late far out of order gone:
   So *Venus* eeke, that goodly Paragone,
   Though faire all night, yet is she darke all day;
   And *Phœbus* self, who lightsome is alone,
   Yet is he oft eclipsed by the way,   3050
And fills the darkned world with terror and dismay.

52

Now *Mars* that valiant man is changed most:
   For, he some times so far runs out of square,
   That he is his way doth seem quite to have lost,
   And cleane without his usuall sphere to fare;   3055
   That even these Star-gazers stonisht are
   At sight thereof, and damne their lying bookes:
   So likewise, grim Sir *Saturne* oft doth spare
   His sterne aspect, and calme his crabbed lookes:
So many turning cranks these have, so many crookes.   3060

53

But you *Dan Iove*, that only constant are,
   And King of all the rest, as ye do clame,
   Are you not subiect eeke to this misfare?
   Then let me aske you this withouten blame,
   Where were ye borne? some say in *Crete* by name,   3065
   Others in *Thebes*, and others other-where;
   But wheresoever they comment the same,
   They all consent that ye begotten were,
And borne here in this world, ne other can appeare.

Ms

54

Then are ye mortall borne, and thrall to me,   3070
   Unlesse the kingdome of the sky yee make
   Immortall, and unchangeable to bee;
   Besides, that power and vertue which ye spake,
   That ye here worke, doth many changes take,
   And your owne natures change: for, each of you.   3075
   That vertue have, or this, or that to make,
   Is checkt and changed from his nature trew,
By others opposition or obliquid view.

55

Besides, the sundry motions of your Spheares,
   So sundry waies and fashions as clerkes faine,   3080
   Some in short space, and some in longer yeares;
   What is the same but alteration plaine?
   Onely the starrie skie doth still remaine:
   Yet do the Starres and Signes therein still move,
   And even it self is mov'd, as wizards saine.   3085
   But all that moveth, doth mutation love:
Therefore both you and them to me I subiect prove.

56

Then since within this wide great *Universe*
   Nothing doth firme and permanent appeare,
   But all things tost and turned by transverse: 3090
   What then should let, but I aloft should reare
   My Trophee, and from all, the triumph beare?
   Now iudge then (O thou greatest goddesse trew!)
   According as thy selfe doest see and heare,
   And unto me addoom that is my dew;   3095
That is the rule of all, all being rul'd by you.

57

So having ended, silence long ensewed,
  Ne *Nature* to or fro spake for a space,
  But with firme eyes affixt, the ground still viewed.
  Meane while, all creatures, looking in her face,   3100
  Expecting th'end of this so doubtfull case,
  Did hang in long suspence what would ensew,
  To whether side should fall the soveraigne place:
  At length, she looking up with chearefull view,
The silence brake, and gave her doome in speeches few.   3105

58

I well consider all that ye have sayd,
  And find that all things stedfastnes doe hate
  And changed be: yet being rightly wayd
  They are not changed from their first estate;
  But by their change their being doe dilate: 3110
  And turning to themselves at length againe,
  Doe worke their owne perfection so by fate:
  Then over them Change doth not rule and raigne;
But they raigne over change, and doe their states maintaine.

59

Cease therefore daughter further to aspire,   3115
  And thee content thus to be rul'd by me:
  For thy decay thou seekst by thy desire;
  But time shall come that all shall changed bee,
  And from thenceforth, none no more change shall see.
  So was the *Titaness* put downe and whist,   3120
  And *Iove* confirm'd in his imperiall see.
  Then was that whole assembly quite dismist,
And *Natur's* selfe did vanish, whither no man wist.

The VIII. Canto, unperfite

1

When I bethinke me on that speech whyleare,
  Of *Mutability*, and well it way: 3125
  Me seemes, that though she all unworthy were
  Of the Heav'ns Rule; yet very sooth to say,
  In all things else she beares the greatest sway.
  Which makes me loath this state of life so tickle,
  And love of things so vaine to cast away;   3130
  Whose flowring pride, so fading and so fickle,
Short *Time* shall soon cut down with his consuming sickle.

2

Then gin I thinke on that which Nature sayd,
  Of that same time when no more *Change* shall be,
  But stedfast rest of all things firmely stayd   3135
  Upon the pillours of Eternity,
  That is contrayr to *Mutabilitie*:
  For, all that moveth, doth in *Change* delight:
  But thence-forth all shall rest eternally
  With Him that is the God of Sabbaoth hight: 3140
O that great Sabbaoth God, graunt me that Sabaoths sight.

NOTES

THE SHEPHEARDES CALENDER (TENTH ECLOGUE). Published in 1579, the *Shepheardes Calender* was at once recognized as a landmark in the development of a national poetry, and it has maintained this reputation in spite of the modern distaste for pastoral eclogues. Nowadays there may be few readers who claim to enjoy the whole work, but it is still read, not only as a preparation for *The Faerie Queene* but because of its own historical importance. It is very ambitiously designed. There is an eclogue for each month, starting (unusually, since the Elizabethan year normally began in March) with January. The eclogues are learned poetry in the pastoral kind as the Renaissance understood it. E. K. (whose identity is not known)[1] provides a humanistic commentary with rhetorical, linguistic and mythological notes. These glosses are sometimes odd; E. K. professes not to understand various allusions, including some that seem obvious. There is some deliberate mystery-making here, not uncharacteristic of Spenser and his time.

Spenser intends to make a new English poetry. Following the example of the French he experiments with obsolete words (some of which he succeeded in reviving). This preoccupation is only partly explained by the tradition that pastoral uses a rustic or 'Doric' dialect, for some of this language remains in the heroic *Faerie Queene*; but that was the part of the work which Sidney, to whom it is dedicated, disapproved. Like Sidney in the *Arcadia*, Spenser also tried out a great variety of English metres and stanza forms, though refraining from the classical experiments in which he has been interested first by Harvey and later by Sidney. His ultimate model was Theocritus: his ambitions were like those of Virgil, who passed from eclogues to epic; and his nearest exemplars were the Italian neo-Latin poet Mantuan and the French poet Marot.

Spenser constructed his poem on a devious scheme. E. K. divides the eclogues into three groups, Plaintive, Recreational, Moral; and though the classification is not obviously right, he properly distinguishes as Moral ('Mixed with some satyricall bitternesse') the second, fifth, seventh, ninth, and tenth ('of contempt of poetrie and pleasaunt wits'). Somewhere in the sequence there is the ghost of a story. Colin

[1] The most likely candidate is Harvey.

Clout is Spenser, Hobbinol is Harvey, and Rosalind, judging from E. K. and Harvey's correspondence, was a real person, but we do not know who; and the love-story is a series of fleeting allusions. It must be remembered, however, that by nature and tradition the pastoral genre was allegorical, aiming, in Puttenham's words, 'under the vaile of homely persons, and in rude speeches to insinuate and glaunce at greater matters'. (He cites Virgil as authority for this.) And *The Shepheardes Calender* undoubtedly deals, under its pastoral veil, with greater matters. Whether or no Rosalind and Dido are Elizabeth herself, Lobbin in the November Eclogue certainly seems to be Leicester; and the 'meeke, wise' shepherd Roffyn of September is Spenser's erstwhile employer Bishop Young, as Algrind is Grindal. This does not exhaust the probable or certain identifications. Spenser followed the Renaissance tradition of using pastoral for ecclesiastical allegory, especially for comment on corruption in the pastors, and *The Shepheardes Calender* contains much comment on the religious issues of the time, generally made from the moderate 'Anglican' point of view which he was always to hold. It may also, even more daringly, reflect the political situation, which was dominated at the time when Spenser was writing, rewriting and revising, by the threatened marriage of the Queen to Alençon. (Spenser certainly alluded to this in *Mother Hubberds Tale*.) Thus the poem, like *The Faerie Queene*, combines great formal complexity with an extremely close application to the important moment in time when the poet was composing.

October, by which the work is here represented, is not political or ecclesiastical. It is primarily, as the Argument says, about poets, poetry, and the neglect of poetry at the time of writing—a traditional complaint, which Spenser was fond of making. Poetry is represented, in accordance with the Renaissance Platonic habit, as divinely inspired: 'no arte, but a divine gift and heavenly instinct'. The poem, as E. K. suggests, is based in part on Mantuan's fifth Eclogue: he also cites Theocritus' *Idyll* xvi, on a ruler's niggardliness to poets.

Argument. Cuddie: E. K. doubts 'whether by Cuddie be specified the authour selfe, or some other'. McLane (see Select Bibliography) proposes the court poet Dyer, friend of Sidney. He can hardly be Spenser, to whom (as Colin) he defers in l. 88.

ἐνθουσιασμός: *enthousiasmos*, the divine fury transporting the poet beyond himself.

the English Poete: Spenser's lost treatise.

Pierce: Piers; perhaps the bishop, perhaps merely an aspect of Spenser.

2. *cast*: plan. *chace*: hunt.

3. *Phoebus race*: the daily course of the sun.

4. *Whilome*: formerly.

5. *bydding base*: a country game.

7. *erst*: lately.

8. *Oten reedes*: pipes. *bene* are. *wore*: worn (out).

9. *spared*: saved.

12. *ligge so layd*: lie so dispiritedly.

12. *dapper*: neat, pretty. *wont*: used to.

14. *fry*: swarm.

15. *what . . . thy?*: how am I the better off for that?

16. *sclender prise*: slender reward.

19 ff. Piers argues for the moral value of poetry and its power over the hearer's soul.

23. *pricke*: spur. *vaine*: poetic vein.

24. 'Wherever you want to lure their captured desires.'

26. *routes*: crowds.

27. *sence bereave*: E. K.'s gloss cites the classic instances of music's power to do this.

28. *shepheard*: Orpheus. *dame*: Eurydice.

30. *hellish hound*: Cerberus.

32. Argus: killed while watching over Jove's mistress Io, having been lulled asleep by Mercury; Juno transferred his hundred eyes to the peacock's tail.

35. *sike*: such. *wasten*: waste.

37 ff. Piers counsels him to write heroic poetry for the court.

39. *giusts*: jousts, tournaments.

40. *weld*: bear. *awful*: awe-inspiring.

41. *doubted*: feared.

42. *wexen*: grow. *woundlesse*: 'doe rust through long peace' (E. K.).

45. Elisa: The Queen.

47–8. *the worthy . . .* : the Earl of Leicester, whose arms are described in l. 48.

49. *stounds*: blows.

50. *slackt*: 'when thou changest thy verse from stately discourse, to matter of more pleasaunce and delight' (E. K.).

52. *Myllers rounde*: 'a kind of daunce' (E. K.).

53. *All were* Elisa: as if Eliza were. *ring*: 'company of dauncers' (E. K.).

54. *mought*: might.

55. *the Romish* Tityrus: 'wel knowen to be Virgile, who by Mecaenas means was brought into favour of the Emperor Augustus, and by him moved to write in loftier kinde, than he erst had doen' (E. K.). Virgil passed from eclogues and georgics to the epic *Aeneid*.

59. *eft*: afterwards.

63. *liggen*: lie.

65. *in derring doe*: 'in manhoode and chevalrie' (E. K.). 'He sheweth the cause, why Poetes were wont to be held in such honor of noble men; that is, that by them their worthines and valor shold through theyr famous Posies be commended to al posterities' (E. K.). He goes on to list stock examples of heroes whose fame was assured by poets: Achilles, Alexander, etc.

69. *pease*: pea (i.e. of no value).

70. *put in preace*: put into practice.

71. *The*: then.

72. *coupe*: cage, prison.

75. *Or*: either. *mote*: must.

76. 'Wallow with all the others in licentious poetry.'

78. *Tom Piper*: name for rustic musician who accompanied morris dancing.

87. *peeced*: imperfect. *bene . . . plight*: are in no condition to do so.

88. *For . . . fittes*: 'It is more appropriate for Colin Clout . . . .'

88. *bedight*: afflicted.

90. *soote as Swanne*: sweetly as the (dying) swan.

91. *fon*: fool.

93. *immortall mirrhor*: 'Beauty, which is an excellent obiect of Poeticall spirites' (E. K.).,

95. *a caytive corage*: 'a base and abiect minde' (E. K.).

100. *vacant*: carefree.

101. *wont*: is accustomed.

102. *weaves*: (he) weaves.

103. *casts to compass*: aspires to achieve.

108. *Wine*: With this figure Spenser resumes the theme of the inspiration necessary to poetry.

113. *bus-kin*: the high boot emblematic of tragedy.

114. *queint* Bellona: 'strange Bellona; the goddesse of battaile, that is Pallas' (E. K.).

116. *For thy*: therefore.

117. *tydes*: times.

118. *charme*: play.

119. *Gates*: goats. *han*: have.

Emblem: from Ovid *Fasti* 6. 5, *est deus in nobis, agitante calescimus illo*—
'there is a god in us, and by his influence we are inspired'. This line
was in frequent use when the divine inspiration of poetry was
discussed.

COLIN CLOUTS COME HOME AGAINE (ll. 835–94). As De Sélincourt
observes, this poem is 'idealized autobiography' in pastoral form.
Published in 1595, it must have been written in 1591 after Spenser's
return to Ireland from the visit to London during which the first three
books of *The Faerie Queene* were published; the lines referring to
Raleigh's disgrace (164–75) are presumably a later insertion. Spenser as
Colin tells Hobbinol and his other shepherd friends of his journey and
sojourn at Cynthia's court. First the Shepherd of the Ocean (Raleigh)
sought him out, and they piped (read their poems) to one another.
Then Raleigh persuaded him to go and see Cynthia, the Queen. Colin
describes the sea and the ship, the strange country over the sea and its
beauties. 'There learned arts do flourish in great honor,/And Poets
wits are held in peerlesse price' (320–1). Cynthia, who approved of his
piping, had other poets, of whom Colin speaks sometimes under
pastoral names (not all of which can be deciphered) and sometimes
openly (Alabaster, Daniel). Then he describes her ladies and her bounty,
which will preserve from oblivion his poor tribute to her. But he
leaves the court because of its wickedness and ambition (though there
are good men there, such as Lobbin-Leicester). A shepherd asks if there
is love at court as well as in the country, and Colin's answer, that
love is blasphemed at court, is commended by Cuddie for its 'deep
insight' into the nature of love; this stimulates Colin to speak the lines
given in this extract. Finally he remembers his old and continuing
love for Rosalind; evening comes on, and they put their sheep to
rest.

Colin Clouts Come Home Againe has abandoned most of the experimental diction of *Shepheardes Calender*, and is much commended as an
example of a familiar style which can still rise to eloquence. It is dedicated to Raleigh in 'part paiment of the infinite debt' Spenser owes
him, and its most obvious interest, after its value as poetry, derives
from the autobiographical element and its allusions to other poets. The
passage here extracted has a special interest for the student of Spenser.
Like the *Hymn in Honour of Love*, it provides a rather formal account
of the Platonic doctrine of love as the power that binds and moves the

whole world. Whether Spenser for the most part adopted these doctrines from medieval sources, or was familiar with the more sophisticated versions of them that had become current in Italy and in France, is a matter of some dispute; but it cannot be denied that in this and similar passages we are given an insight into a very important aspect of Spenser's imaginative thinking. Here love is represented as the heavenly power that made the world, resolved the contraries of chaos (hot and cold, moist and dry, &c.), ordered the elements, and generally arranged a creative coincidence of opposites, of which generative love is a type. Thus the earth was filled with animal life. But men, having reason, are guided not merely by passion but by a desire for beauty; and those who dishonour this ennobling love are condemned as lustful and outlawed by the god.

839. *y'bore*: born.

843. *attone*: agreement.

849. *peize*: press heavily down.

850. *voydnesse*: emptiness.

851. *wexed*: became.

855. *gan*: began.

859. *wight*: creature.

862. *kindly*: natural. *formall feature*: shape.

876. *no*: nor. *ward*: protect oneself against.

878. *stownd*: blow.

884. *saw*: command.

887. *deeme*: judge, believe.

890. *lore*: teaching.

894: *Exuls*: exiles.

EPITHALAMION (published with *Amoretti* in 1595). Although Spenser's sonnet sequence, the *Amoretti*, uses many of the conventional themes and figures, it has a strongly personal quality. For instance, it alludes to the writing of *The Faerie Queene* (xxxiii, lxxx), to his friend Bryskett, to his mother, and above all to his courtship of Elizabeth Boyle and her final acceptance of him. The long *Epithalamion*, which crowns the volume, shows the same blend of convention and intimate personal application. Though in the classics the bridegroom is never the singer, it is based on the classical marriage-song, of which the sixty-first and sixty-second *carmina* of Catullus are probably the most familiar examples; and it mentions ceremonies more appropriate to a Roman than to an Irish wedding (compare Jonson's wedding masque *Hymenaei*, where there are learned notes on these customs, or the later epithalamion of Herrick). With the pagan imagery so introduced, Spenser without apology blends Christian figures, in the tradition of the High Renaissance. The division of the poem into long and apparently irregular stanzas is, in part, Spenser's way of adapting to English taste the stricter Italian *canzone*; neither in rhyme-scheme nor in length are they strictly related, and the impression of easily ordered abundance is reinforced by the many variations introduced into the refrain.

Epithalamion is the climax of Spenser's lyrical art, not merely in this lightly-controlled and mellifluous abundance, but in its power to convey great and ordered joy, the *genial* power of married love (using *genial* in the sense it has in the poem). The climax is in pure physical pleasure and the desire of that generation which, as *Colin Clout* and the *Hymns* assure us, is the good purpose of the earthly Venus, and which makes more souls for heaven.

The poem moves with such ease, and might seem so simply to follow in its structure the events of the wedding-day, that it may be a surprise to the reader to discover that it has a remarkably elaborate secret design. Spenser shared the interest of many medieval and Renaissance poets in numerological patterns, and Mr. A. Kent Hieatt has recently shown that *Epithalamion* contains a very elaborate example of this kind of writing. It has twenty-three stanzas and the envoy: one for each hour of the day. The date of the wedding is the summer solstice; the stanzas representing hours of daylight on that day in the latitude of southern Ireland have refrains based on 'The woods shall to me answer', whereas the refrain for the hours of darkness is 'The woods no more shall answer'. There are 365 long lines in the poem, one for each day of the year. For other evidence of the strict design underlying this apparently free-moving poem, see Professor Kent's book (details in Select Bibliography). It is of course true that generations of readers have admired what C. S. Lewis called the 'festal sublimity' of *Epithalamion* without suspecting this pattern; but it tells us something about Spenser. Other minor poems also have numerological patterns (e.g. *Daphnaida* and *The Ruines of Time*) and it is becoming clear that *The Faerie Queene* also has extremely complicated patterns of this kind.[1]

[1] See A. D. S. Fowler, 'Numerical Composition in *The Faerie Queene*', *Journal of the Warburg and Courtauld Institutes*, xxv (1962), pp. 199–239, now developed at greater length in his *Spenser and the Numbers of Time* (London, 1964).

184 NOTES

We may see them as more important to the writer than the reader. For him they represented a way of reproducing as a poet should the greater order of God's creation, itself numerically regular; and in *Epithalamion* they helped him to make his own love appear as a genuine type of the creative force that made the world.

1. *learned sisters*: the muses.

3. *graceful*: conferring grace.

7. *list*: desired.

22. *lusty hed*: vigour.

25. *Hymen*: god of marriage.

26. *mask*: procession of dancers.

27. *Tead*: torch. *flake*: flash.

30. *dight*: dress.

33. *usury*: interest.

39. *sea . . . neare*: Elizabeth Boyle had been staying at Youghal, an Irish port.

40. *beseene*: provided.

48. *whereas*: where.

51. *diapred*: dotted with flowers. *discolored*: variously coloured.

56. *Mulla*: the river Awbeg, which flows near Kilcolman.

75. *Tithones*: the husband of Aurora, the dawn.

82. *Ouzel*: blackbird. *Ruddock*: robin.

87. *make*: mate.

95. *Hesperus*: the morning star.

98. *houres*: the *horai*, or hours, were daughters of Day (i.e. Jove) and Night.

103. *three . . . Queene*: the Graces and Venus.

108. *use*: customarily do.

118. *lifull*: life-bestowing.

123. *mote . . . delight*: may have delighted.

131. *Croud*: fiddle.

132. *iar*: discord.

140. *Hymen io Hymen*: the classical marriage-cry.

148. *portly*: stately.

149. *Phoebe*: the moon.

152. *beseemes*: becomes. *weene*: think.

173. *rudded*: reddened.

175. *uncrudded*: uncurdled.

186. *spright*: spirit.

189. *red*: saw.

190. *Medusaes*: Medusa was the gorgon whose appearance turned men to stone. *mazeful*: confounding.

196. *affections*: emotions.

206. *doth behove*: is fitting.

228. *in grayne*: thoroughly.

239. *band*: bond.

266. *Barnaby*: St. Barnabas, on whose day (11 June, then the longest day) the marriage took place.

269. *Crab*: Zodiacal sign of Cancer.

275. *bonefiers*: bonfires (more usual on St. John's Eve, 23 June).

282. *Planet*: the sun.

290. *nightes*: (a disyllable.)

296. *forepast*: past, done with.

307. *Maia*: who bore Jove Hermes, after the encounter described.

316. *defray*: pay for.

328–9. *Iove . . . groome*: Hercules was the child of Alcmena by Jove.

331. *Maiesty*: Spenser appears to have invented this myth of Majesty as the child of Jove by Night.

339. *helpelesse*: beyond cure.

341. *Pouke*: puck, hobgoblin.

345. *shriech Oule*: screech-owl, whose cry forboded death.

356. *playne*: complaint.

374. *Cinthia*: the moon. Perhaps with an allusion to Queen Elizabeth, called Cynthia.

376: *envy*: be jealous, resent.

380. *Latmian shepherd*: Endymion, beloved of Cynthia.

390. *Iune*: patroness of marriage.

392. *religion*: rites. *plight*: pledged.

395. *smart*: labour.

398. *Genius*: patron of the marriage ('geniall') bed, presiding over generation.

405. *Hebe*: Spenser allocates these 'genial' duties to the divine handmaiden, who does not have them in antiquity.

433. 'Though the time described is brief (a day) commemorate it for ever.'

THE FAERIE QUEENE. For general remarks on *The Faerie Queene*, see Introduction, pp. 17–26, *The Letter to Raleigh*. Written after Spenser's return to London with Raleigh in 1589 (the date given is Old Style, and means 1590), this letter was appended to the first three books of *The Faerie Queene* in the volume of 1590. It presents certain problems;

for example, the account of Book II (ll. 152 ff.) seems to conflict with the poem as we have it. Also the reference to 'the twelve private morall vertues, as Aristotle hath devised' (38–40) and the subsequent mention of Magnificence and 'the xii. other vertues' (88) has caused long controversy; how far is Spenser following the *Nicomachean Ethics*, which has no list of twelve virtues, and in any case does not fit the six which Spenser actually treated? (For example, Temperance is an Aristotelian virtue, Holiness is not.) The error in the story of Guyon must be attributed to Spenser's deliberately setting down in the Letter that part of it which he had not treated in the poem; perhaps in haste, he omitted to make it minutely consistent with the rest. As to the virtues, it is possible that he thought of the *Ethics* (or some Christian commentary upon them) merely as providing a *schema*, from which he must understandably vary. In any case, the puzzles of the Letter should not be should not be allowed to obscure its value as an aid to understanding the poem. Its argument may be summarized thus:

1. (1–12) Mode of the work: allegory.

2. (12–44) Moral intention; justification of subject and, by historical precedent, procedures.

3. (44–59) Defence of allegorical narrative poetry as moral agent: 'so much more profitable and gratious is doctrine by ensample, then by rule.'

4. (60–87) 'General intention' in portrayal of Arthur and of the Faerie Queene and the other 'shadowings' of Elizabeth.

5. (87–95) The other knights (first three books).

6. (95–172) Difference between poetry and historiography; stories of the first three books 'historiographically' rendered.

7. (173–178) 'Other adventures intermedled.'

8. (179–187) conclusion: the letter was written to establish general design of a poem that might have seemed, without this aid, 'tedious and confused'.

The Letter is in many respects what might be expected in the way of self-justification by a Renaissance heroic poet, and the advanced student ought to compare it with the discourses of Tasso on heroic poetry and Sidney's *Defence of Poetry*. The poem is a 'darke conceit', but the poet, while valuing darkness, can offer certain guide-ropes. His purpose is the proper and conventional one of fashioning a gentleman; his defence of poetry is that it makes the moral pill pleasanter to swallow. The choice of subject—King Arthur—fits the requirement that the hero should be great and distant in time; he also, as Spenser omits to say, has his important role as official ancestor of the Tudors and the last emperor of all Britain, so complying with the type of hero used by Virgil and the Italians. For the poet's models in this moral activity are the right ones: Homer (interpreted in the manner of contemporary criticism); Virgil (who meant much more to Spenser, and expounded a similarly imperial theme); and the two great modern heroic poets, Ariosto and Tasso, whose sharp distinction between ethical and political ends Spenser professes to follow in the over-all design of his book.

Practising this teaching of 'doctrine by ensample', Spenser chose Arthur; but Arthur could not stand in the same relation to Elizabeth as Aeneas to Augustus, if only because of her sex. He is Magnificence, summing all the Virtues. She is represented (1) as the Faerie Queene, also Glory—that for which a gentleman strives; and (2) in her second 'person' or body natural as opposed to body politic, Belphoebe, 'a most vertuous and beautifull Lady'. (It should be remembered that this by no means accounts for all the figures in the poem which represent Elizabeth.) The other knights, 'for the more variety of the history', represent other virtues. (Spenser does not allude to his obvious difficulty in finding a place in the scheme for the all-virtuous Arthur after granting the several virtues to lesser knights.) There follows the passage in which Spenser tries, not quite successfully, to translate his poetry into the terms of historiography. He confines himself to narrative, but allows us an occasional hint of his allegorical intentions —as when he speaks of Red Cross's armour as that of St. Paul's *miles Christi* (Ephesians vi). The description of certain later episodes as 'Accidents' rather than 'intendments' does not mean that they have no allegorical significance, only that these are secondary to the grand design here outlined.

1. *doubtfully*: ambiguously.

4. *gealous*: hostile, envious.

8. *particular*: as opposed to 'general' in 6; meaning, e.g. the 'accidents' mentioned at the end of the letter.

39–40. *commune sence*: i.e. the lower rather than the higher powers of the soul.

43. *Cyrus*: for the conventional praise of Xenophon's *Cyropadeia*, see Sidney's *Defence of Poetry*.

55–73. *her kingdome in Faery land*: i.e. 'by the Faery land of the poem I mean England'.

57. *two persons*: a reference to the legal doctrine which held that the monarch was in two persons, called her body politic ('Queene or

Empresse') and her body natural ('most vertuous and beautifull Lady').

   79. *into the middest*: in medias res, as Horace (*Ars Poetica*, 148) advises.

   89. *clownishe*: countrified, rustic.

103. *Presently*: at once.

106. *gainesaying*: protesting.

111. *furnitures*: equipment.

133–4. *intermedled*: mixed in.

138. *overronne*: run over.

141. *gripe*: grip.

141. *happily*: perhaps.

Faerie Queene I. It is unlikely that Spenser composed his poem straight through, beginning at I. i; and the opening we know cannot be what Harvey saw in 1580. But whenever he composed Book I, he worked to a detailed plan. No other book, even II, is so nearly self-contained. Its hero is the greatest of the knights, a saint rather than a hero; and its historical scope is nothing less than the history of the world from the expulsion of Adam and Eve from Eden to the final overthrow of Satan. It is the most simply religious of the books, yet at the same time it has a sustained and complex allegory; and in no other is Spenser speaking so urgently to the great historical themes as they were understood in his day.

   St. George, the Red Cross Knight, slayer of the dragon, was a figure of folk-play and pageant, still regarded in England as a true saint, and having his regular place in such celebrations as those which annually marked the Queen's Birthday. He walks into Spenser's opening stanzas with his usual companions, the lady riding on her ass, and the lamb; and his story is chivalric, according to the fashion revived during the time of Elizabeth and reflected in much literature, high and low, of the period. The landscape against which we see Red Cross in the famous opening stanzas is shadowy, dreamlike—not Britain, not any-where else; and we see what Coleridge meant when he spoke of 'the marvellous independence and true imaginative absence of all particular space and time' in *The Faerie Queene*. But what we have to learn is that this is, paradoxically, a serviceable milieu—that these characters from the village play and the Lord Mayor's Show are, paradoxically, suitable agents—and that a story of dreamlike transfigurations, of nightmare apparitions and meanings that glow momentarily out of a dark ground are the proper medium for a narrative that bears acutely on the human condition, and upon the history of mankind as it seemed to culminate in the late 1580's. This is the sense in which Spenser's is an heroic poem: it treats, as does Virgil's, of human destiny in the context of earthly empire and divine providence.

Red Cross, though of the elect, is a sinner, everyman; his fall into sin and despair Spenser emphasizes by repeating the anti-Romanist teaching of his church: 'that we are justified by faith alone is a most wholesome doctrine'. But he repents, undertakes the imitation of Christ, and finally, when he redeems the parents of Una, he defeats the old dragon and harrows hell—becomes, in short, Christ, the object of his imitation. These are the strange transformations of Spenser's world; and they are prepared for in the opening lines. For Red Cross, who wears his 'bloudie Crosse' in memory of his Lord, is also called 'Right faithfull true'. The victor over Satan in medieval illuminated Apocalypses wore the Red Cross; he was the warrior 'faithful and true' of Revelation, Christ himself. And Red Cross was also England.

To understand this, one has to grasp the simple fact that the Book of Revelation is the principal source of *Faerie Queene* I. Una is 'the woman clothed with the sun', traditionally identified as the true Church; Spenser, remembering her as this, speaks of 'her sunshyny face', just as the medieval illuminators showed her in a glory of sunlight. Duessa, though she is primarily multiplicity, the opposite of Una's integrity, is also the Whore of Babylon, and the best illustrations of Spenser's eighth canto, where she rides the beast with seven heads, are in the old illuminated Apocalypses. Archimago is antichrist, a character associated with the Beast from the Land in Revelation. The tree and the water, representing the two sacraments of the reformed Church (communion and baptism) refresh Red Cross during his three-day battle with the dragon; they come from Revelation xxii. And so forth.

Now the Book of Revelation was held to contain in prophetic form the history of the Church; and the interpretation favoured by Spenser was Protestant and Anglican. The true Catholic church was the church of England; and Una is therefore that Church, and in some respects its head, the empress who gave it strength to live again: Elizabeth. Since Archimago, the antichrist, represents the papacy, and Duessa the corrupt Roman church, the restoration of both true religion and the original Christian empire in England is a type of the restoration of Eden.

Thus Spenser embodies in his dream the imperial and ecclesiastical pretensions of the last Tudor. By means of his 'cloudy' allegorical

Ns

techniques he associates the reigning monarch with a triumphant *renovatio* of the true church, and of the empire whose beginnings Virgil had celebrated in the *Aeneid*. In doing so, he does not choose materials of an intrinsically courtly or difficult kind; rather he builds into his heroic pattern the familiar figures of Revelation, and of the mummer's play, and he calls upon universal history to justify the worship of the imperial Elizabeth. Not surprisingly, in the words of Colin Clout, she 'gan take delight' when she listened to his poem, 'And it desir'd at timely hours to hear.'

Canto i, 1–27. Spenser introduces the knight and his quest; then the lady and her attendants: the lamb signifying her purity, the dwarf her reluctant human part. She is the daughter of humanity as it was before the fall, the universal Church—not like Duessa (ii. 22), merely of the church of Rome. When it rains they seek shelter in a wood. It is the wood of error, or, like the wood at the beginning of Dante's *Inferno*, of human existence. The Lady cautions her knight against over-confidence in his unaided strength; but, unheeding, he provokes, then fights with, Error. Error is heresy, corrupter of true doctrine in England as elsewhere. Redcross is in difficulties: 'Add faith unto your force,' cries the lady, stating a tenet of the true religion; his natural strength is useless alone. Error spews out its brood of heresy, but the knight triumphs.

This victory, like the victory of Christ over Satan in the wilderness, prefigures later success with the old dragon; but his earlier lapse equally foretells the terrible sins that lie ahead of Red Cross. Whether or no Spenser intended Error to stand for all those early heresies which first plagued the church, he certainly contrived to make his first canto an emblem of the whole book, as the book in a sense contains all the rest of the poem. And one observes that for all his 'sweetness' and remoteness, Spenser can make evil things sound disagreeable.

Immediately after this episode Red Cross encounters Archimago who takes him home and, by producing an evil spirit falsely representing Una, succeeds in separating the knight and his charge.

1. *pricking*: spurring.

5. *never*: because (see Letter to Raleigh) these arms were not his, but another's, given him by the Faery Queene. They were, in fact, the defences of Christ against temptation.

18. *ydrad*: dreaded.

19. *bond*: bound.

31. *wimpled*: folded.

52. *Leman*: mistress.

53. *shrowd*: shelter.

69 ff. *The sayling Pine*, &c.: This catalogue of trees is epic in origin, though probably developed here from Chaucer's *Parlement of Foules*.

84. *weening*: intending.

87. *weene*: think.

116. *read*: counsel.

129. *boughtes*: bends.

134. *uncouth*: unfamiliar.

136. *effraide*: scared.

139. *entraile*: entanglement.

141. *to point*: fully.

142. *bale*: fire.

147. *trenchand*: sharp.

152. *enhaunst*: raised.

154. *dint*: blow.

158. *Tho*: then.

175. *vildly*: vilely.

180. *parbreake*: vomit.

185. *avale*: sink.

189. *reed*: see.

200. *Phoebus*: the sun. *welke*: fade.

201. *vewen*: view, survey.

208. *bestedd*: placed.

212. *lin*: cease.

227. *Impes*: young, children.

239. *Armorie*: armour.

Book I, Canto ii, 20–26. Red Cross, parted from Una, meets the pagan Sansfoy with Duessa. They fight; Sansfoy, cursing the bloody Cross, dies. These stanzas describe Duessa's behaviour at the death of her champion.

Naturally, her account of her past is false, but what she says of her parentage (22) should be compared with Una's account of hers (i. 5). Her union with Sansfoy ('without faith') signifies an unholy alliance of Rome with the antichrist of Islam—the principal enemies of Christendom. Sansloy, a brother, is killed in Book II, the book of Temperance; Sansjoy in Book III, the book of Chastity. They form a sort of pagan counterpart to Faith, Hope, and Charity (Fidelia, Speranza,

Charissa in canto x), and each is overcome by the appropriate Virtue.

Red Cross believes 'Fidessa's' story, despite the warning of Fradubio— now turned into a tree (captive to sin)—who had fallen in just the same way to the wiles of Duessa. The canto deals not only with Red Cross's human lapse into sin, but with the desertion of the original true faith by England.

248. *scowre*: run.

260. *rueth*: causes me to pity.

Book I, Canto iv, 17–37. The third canto describes Una, under the protection of a lion (standing for something like 'natural reverence for truth') as she shelters in the House of blind Devotion (the Roman faith, attended by superstition and clerical greed). She is joined by Archimago disguised as Red Cross (masquerading as the protector of true religion). Archimago is defeated in fight by the pagan Sansloy, who kills the lion and takes Una captive. In iv, Duessa leads the true Red Cross into the House of Pride, presided over by Lucifera (Pride) and six counsellors representing the other deadly sins. The famous pageant of the Seven Deadly Sins is given in this extract. It is a characteristic Spenserian exercise in a standard allegorical topic; much of the detail is conventional, but it is handled with energy and originality. After it, Red Cross is challenged by Sansjoy, the third of the unholy brothers, to whose cause Duessa rallies. The Canto is primarily concerned with the knight's fall into sin; Sansjoy is the first representative of Despair, the sinner's hopelessness of bliss.

307. *she*: i.e. Lucifera.

309. Flora . . . *prime*: the goddess of flowers in springtime.

314. *Pecocks*: birds sacred to June.

315. Argus *eyes*: see *Shepheardes Calender* Oct. l. 32.

319. 'given as appropriate to the nature of each.'

323. *amis*: hood, cape.

325. *Portesse*: breviary.

331. *wayne*: wagon, pageant.

334. *esloyne*: remove.

336. *essoyne*: excuse.

372. *whally*: green-tinged.

378. *fantasy*: fancy.

382. *new fangleness*: novelty of fashion.

406. *yplast*: placed.

410. *compare*: acquire.

NOTES 193

425. *still*: continually.

433. *kirtle*: tunic. *Say*: Serge.

437. *implyes*: enfolds.

439. *griple*: grasping.

443. *that . . . use*: that did such deeds.

459. *choler*: the bodily humour that causes anger.

462. *unadvized*: unreflecting. *wood*: mad.

464. *car'd for*: cared about (spilling).

466. *facts*: deeds.

471. *scath*: injury.

476. *Saint Fraunces fire*: erysipelas.

477. *tire*: train.

Book I, Canto vii, 29–33. In Canto v Red Cross defeats Sansjoy: but Duessa saves his life and conveys him to Aesculapius in hell, where he is healed. By the help of the Dwarf, Red Cross perceives the dangers of the House of Pride, and they leave. Canto vi tells how Una is rescued from Sansloy by a band of satyrs who, in 'bootlesse zeale', worship her ass when she forbids them to worship her. Sir Satyrane, son of a lady by a savage man, arrives on the scene, admires Una's sacred wisdom, and enables her to flee. Archimago tells them that Sansloy has killed Red Cross, and Sansloy appears to fight with Satyrane. Una escapes. (This is one of Spenser's loose ends; Satyrane's fight is never concluded; he turns up again in III. vii. 28, quite a different context.) The satyrs stand for natural religion, perhaps, as it was evinced in the extremist movements of early reform; Satyrane for a good blend of nature and civility, which can receive the truth—like the reformed Church of England.

In canto vii, Red Cross is tricked by Duessa into drinking of an enervating fountain; he has removed his Pauline armour, and the water has the opposite effect of that in canto xii (baptism). While he is powerless he is taken prisoner by Orgoglio, the Pride of Life, a great enemy of holiness. Orgoglio's mistress is Duessa in her role as Whore of Babylon, wearing the triple crown of the papacy. The Dwarf finds Una and reports these happenings. As she laments, Prince Arthur comes upon them, and the extract is part of Spenser's first description of his super-hero. It is a development in chivalric language of the account of the angel in Revelation xviii; the stone of 30 is drawn from the seal of the spouse in Canto viii. 6. Spenser's plan is, roughly, to have Arthur intervene in the seventh or eighth canto of each book; so it is in

I, II, and V. Una tells him of her plight (her parents have been the captive of the dragon for four years—i.e. 4,000 years, the time between the fall of Adam and the birth of Christ) and Red Cross is in danger. Arthur promises help.

499. *glitterand*: glittering.

503. *bauldrick*: girdle.

511. *slights*: devices.

527–8. These lines are imitated either from or by Marlowe in 1 *Tamburlaine* IV. iv.

Book I, Canto ix, 45–54. In the eighth canto Arthur, here representing divine grace, slays Orgoglio, wounds the beast, and captures Duessa. He enters the castle, hears the blood of the martyrs crying out for vengeance, and discovers Red Cross in a dungeon. Duessa is stripped and shown in all her true ugliness.

Canto ix contains Arthur's story of his love for Gloriana. Arthur and Red Cross exchange gifts of religious import, and they part. Red Cross encounters Sir Terwin, fleeing from the cave of Despair; he goes to the cave and meets Despair, who advises him to end a life which can do him no good and give him no pleasure. The lines of the extract contain a part of his speech. The knight wavers, near to despairing of his own salvation; but Una saves him from suicide, urging that he is among the elect, and may expect grace. Despair unavailingly hangs himself. This is a powerful picture of the dark passages in the life of a saint, or indeed of any man conscious of sin, who seeks and fears not to find grace.

544. *amate*: dismay, amaze.

563. *law*: Despair of course omits to mention the pardon which followed this just sentence.

579. *dant*: daunt.

590. *overcraw*: exult over.

596. *raught*: handed.

605. *crudled*: curdled.

608. *rife*: deeply.

610. *reprochfull*: worthy of reproach.

619. *brond*: brand, ember.

622. *amounted*: mounted.

623. *carle*: churl.

Book I, Canto x, 46–68. In this canto Una brings Red Cross to the

House of Holiness, where he will meet Fidelia, Speranza, and Charissa, daughters of Caelia (Heaven). The 'soule-diseased knight' undergoes severe penance and undertakes, in an allegory of seven headsmen in a hospital, the seven corporal works of mercy. He is thus prepared for Contemplation, and there follows the passage extracted. Contemplation leads Red Cross to the top of a holy mountain, compared to both Sinai and the Mount of Olives, and even to Parnassus, haunt of the Muses. From this height he sees the Heavenly Jerusalem, and can compare it with its earthly counterpart, Cleopolis (London). Contemplation now gives Red Cross his saint's name, and accounts for his association with England. The knight reluctantly leaves, to bring his quest to an end.

644. *persant*: piercing.

679. *aread*: show.

692. *bands*: bonds. *assoiled*: released.

695. *man of God*: Moses.

698. *yod*: went.

710. *thrise . . . Ladies*: the nine Muses.

730. *Hierusalem*: the Heavenly Jerusalem of Hebrews xii. 22–33.

737. *sam*: together.

744. *Panthea*: presumably a royal palace, perhaps Greenwich.

757. *ymp*: child, offspring.

760. *foredonne*: undone.

763. *shonne*: shun, avoid.

779. *faine*: willing (to abandon).

783. *are*: i.e. they are.

788. *empare*: diminish.

790. *that . . . care*: i.e. the charge of that royal maid which has been entrusted to you.

792. *quit*: delivered.

794. *abet*: uphold.

797. *aread*: advise, explain.

798. *behight*: call.

800. *avouchen*: prove, establish.

807. *unweeting*: unknown to you.

816. *Georgos*: in Greek, a farmer or ploughman.

870. *quight*: requite.

830. *cast*: resolved.

Book I, Canto xi, 29–34, 46–48. The eleventh canto is devoted to the battle of the Red Cross Knight with the Dragon. The first day's combat goes badly for the knight, who finds that in the heat of the battle with evil that the armour of faith becomes intolerable to him; whereupon he is revived by the Well of Life, symbol of baptism. The first extract describes the effect of this well on the almost-defeated knight; he is reborn for the second day's struggle against death. The second day goes better for a time, but the knight is again beaten back, this time to the Tree of Life, which represents the sacrament of the Eucharist. The second extract describes the effect of the Tree, and its power to prepare Red Cross for the third and last day of the fight, in which the dragon is killed. The fight is a type of the victory over Satan in the Last Days: and in the final canto Red Cross, again like Christ, releases souls by harrowing hell, and restores Eden. Like Christ again, he takes Una (the Church) as his bride; the marriage feast, as described, derives from Revelation. Una appears for the first time in her full beauty (as in the Church of England, which restored the ancient church in its purity). Then Archimago turns up with a lying letter from Duessa; but he is exposed and cast bound into a dungeon (Revelation xx). Finally Red Cross, or St. George, resumes his knightly role, and returns to the service of Gloriana for six more years.

843. *Whylome*: once upon a time.

845. *hot*: was called.

852. Silo: the Pool of Siloam.

854. Cephise: Cephisus. Hebrus: river in Thrace, famous for purity of water.

860. *kest*: cast.

866. *assay*: assault.

885. *As Eagle*: referring to the old belief that the eagle renewed its youth by burning off its feathers in the sphere of fire, then plunging into the ocean, whence it emerged with new plumage.

888. *Eyas*: young hawk.

895. *over . . . red*: were told of everywhere.

898. *sted*: place.

900. *the crime*: i.e. accusation; after they had eaten of the Tree of the Knowledge of Good and Evil, God cast Adam and Eve out of Eden for fear they should eat of the Tree of Life, and so grow immortal. The Tree of Knowledge is mentioned in 47. The Knight now has received both sacraments, and can achieve his quest on the third day.

The Faerie Queene, II. Spenser designed the second book as far as possible on the model of the first. His two knights in canto i, and we are told that Guyon has 'like race to runne'. Guyon's early encounter with Amavia, providing 'the whole subject' of the book, is analogous to Red Cross's fight with Error. In the seventh canto Guyon is tempted by Mammon, a crucial passage corresponding in a sense to Red Cross's overthrow by Orgoglio in the seventh canto of Book I. Arthur's rescue effort comes in canto viii. In the ninth canto, Despair is defeated and the beleaguered House of Alma described; in the eleventh, the Dragon and Maleger are overthrown. The final cantos express the true Eden and a false Eden which Guyon destroys. The parallelism is even more extensive than this suggests.

But Book II has nevertheless its independent organization; it is analogous to, rather than dependent upon, Book I. It is the Legend of Temperance; its main theme is the control of human passion by the higher powers of the mind. This virtue discussed by Aristotle in the *Nicomachean Ethics*, where he distinguished between temperance and continence; the former does not, like the latter, presuppose the existence of strong and base desires that have to be overcome. Guyon is a mixture of the two, and it does not seem likely that Spenser tried to keep to Aristotle's scheme. Temperance, after all, was one of the four Cardinal Virtues—the others being Prudence, Fortitude, and Justice—which were borrowed from the ancients by Christian thought, and which with the Theological Virtues (Faith, Hope, and Charity) made up the seven to balance the Deadly Sins. Christian Temperance had its own lore and its own emblems—the setsquare, the bridle, the wine mixed with water, or the mixing-bowl itself—all of which Spenser uses; the very name Guyon derives from that one of the four rivers of Eden—Gehon—which was associated with the virtue. Spenser's was an imagination which developed and added to discrete hints, rather than followed a pre-arranged and inclusive philosophical scheme.

That there are Aristotelian elements, whether copied directly or inherited from a long tradition of moralistic commentary, is nevertheless not to be denied. Aristotle's habitual account of a virtue as a mean between excess and deficiency is important to Spenser, and so is his doctrine that the passions of the body, which temperance and continence oppose, are the angry and the desirous, the irascible and the concupiscible. Spenser repeatedly illustrates this division; he concentrates on the first part of it in the opening six cantos, and on the second in the final six. Even the state to which Guyon ultimately attains—Heroic

Virtue—though it has a theological definition, is also mentioned by Aristotle as the opposite of bestiality.

The conflicts in which Guyon is involved take place in the human being; thus the second book has far less of the supernatural than the first, and is much more concerned with the moral activity of men in the natural world. (Temperance, after all, was a virtue the pagans could recognize; Holiness was known only by revelation to Christians.) The problems of Guyon involve his holding to the golden mean, being neither forward nor 'froward', impatient nor impotent, neither too much nor too little. He has the Palmer, Reason, to aid him, though he does not always use him. He is here much more like a pagan such as Aeneas than Red Cross, who is a saint; and, like Aeneas, he visits the underworld.

This is not to say that Spenser has abandoned Christianity in Book II, nor that he has returned from romance to classical epic. The story of Ruddymane, Amavia, and Mortdant in the first canto is Christian. Mortdant is infected by concupiscence with Original Sin, having succumbed to the desires of the flesh. As his name tells us, he is the 'death-giver', like Adam. The fountain is Divine Law, which provides sin with its occasion to produce concupiscence in men (Romans, vii. 7). The burial of Mortdant and Amavia is that of the Old Man; Ruddy-mane, the bloody babe, is baptized, but still stained by the concupiscence contracted by his father from Acrasia (Incontinence). Guyon at first thinks the tragedy is merely one of intemperance; the Palmer conveys to him its deeper significance in canto ii. The destruction of the Bower of Bliss is not only the destruction of Incontinence, but of sin in the human heart. Spenser builds Temperance into a Christian scheme, just as the theological tradition had done.

Nor does he quite abandon romance. Mammon is borrowed from Celtic folk tale. Acrasia has many analogues in Italian romance epic —Alcina in Ariosto, Armida in Tasso, Acratia in Trissino. Of course the ancestress of them all is Homer's Circe, who was generally read allegorically as providing such men as refused her cup with the chance of Heroic Virtue, and turning those who could not into beasts.

In his quest Guyon achieves Heroic Virtue, and illustrates the part of Temperance in the Christian task of defeating the lust of the flesh, the lust of the eye, and the pride of life. The first canto establishes the nature of this quest; the second offers a schematic representation of the doctrine of the mean, in the House of Medina. She is the mean; her

sisters Elissa (Greek 'deficient') and Perissa (Greek 'excessive') the
extremes. Their lovers share their qualities; Perissa's is Sansloy, the
lawlessness of appetite that Guyon must kill, and does. The third
canto tells of the theft of Guyon's horse by Braggadocchio and introduces Belphoebe into the story; this is an early instalment of the third
book rather than a direct contribution to the second. In the fourth,
Spenser deals with anger and its occasion. Furor is bound with a hundred
chains, Occasio's tongue is locked; there is a tale to illustrate the evil
effects of anger (which Shakespeare borrowed for *Much Ado*). Other
characters are Atin (Strife), Pyrochles ('fire disturbed', incontinent
anger), and Cymochles ('wave disturbed', incontinent sex), who will
be considered later.

In the fifth canto Guyon overthrows Pyrochles, and there are further
instances of anger and its occasions; Atin, seeking out Cymochles to
help his brother, finds him in the Bower of Bliss—another forecast
of the story to come. Canto vi, a transition between the irascible and the
concupiscible, opens with an Aristotelian moralization: 'A Harder lesson,
to learne Continence/ In ioyous pleasure, then in grievous paine', and
places Guyon, without his Palmer, in the hands of the laughing lady
Phaedria (Greek 'glittering', but Spenser himself calls her 'immodest
Merth'). She sails about on the idle lake; and loose mirth floating on
idleness leads, as Spenser observes, to 'loose desire'. Cymochles is Phaedria's thrall, and she sings to him of the beauty and plenty of the false
paradise she inhabits on a floating island. Guyon behaves with correct-
ness, and speaks courteously to Phaedria, but 'her dalliance he despised',
and has small difficulty in resisting her temptations. There follows an in-
conclusive quarrel between Guyon and Cymochles; and the sight of
Pyrochles, trying to drown himself in order to extinguish the fire of
anger within him, saved by Archimago. This is a fine canto, to which
much attention should be given. Phaedria is the agent of Acrasia, but
she is made to seem attractive; Guyon undergoes sensual temptation
without the Palmer's aid, and although he has little difficulty in withstanding it, it is part of a pattern of testing completed in the next canto.
Spenser finely maintains the traits of temperance, such as courtesy
and just anger; and also, in a canto more than usually various, characterizes with delicate strength the concupiscent Cymochles and the
irascible Pyrochles ('Burning in flames, yet no flames can I see,/ And
dying daily, daily yet revive').

The seventh canto is here given in full. It is the crucial part of the
book. Still without his Palmer, Guyon proceeds without difficulty,

reflecting comfortably on his own virtues, through the wilderness. He meets Mammon, 'God of the world and worldlings', of money, fame, and power. Guyon scornfully rejects an attempt to buy him with money, but visits Mammon's underground estates. The allegorical figures on the road to Hell are self-explanatory. Throughout his three-day sojourn below the earth, Guyon is followed by a monstrous fiend that hangs over him, waiting to tear him to pieces if he once wavers. He has no difficulty with riches, having chosen 'another blis . . . another end'. In the Temple of Philotime ('love of [earthly] honour') he is tempted by wordly ambition, but explains that he has plighted his troth to 'another lady'—to the true heavenly glory. Mammon then tempts him in the Garden of Proserpina: this is a temptation to forbidden knowledge. Guyon is unmoved, and Mammon, his time expired, leads him back to the light. There Guyon faints; the eighth canto begins with the famous 'And is there care in heaven?' and the account of an angel sent to succour Guyon.

That this is among the greatest of Spenser's cantos nobody denies; as Lamb said, 'the transitions in this episode are every whit as violent as in the most extravagant dream, and yet the waking judgement ratifies them'. Yet there is much dispute about its interpretation; some think the episode illustrates Guyon's weakness in not avoiding the occasion of temptation. Milton, though he wrongly supposed that the Palmer accompanied Guyon into the cave, is more likely to have been right in speaking of how 'our sage and serious Poet *Spencer* . . . describing true temperance under the person of *Guion*, brings him in with his palmer through the cave of Mammon, and the bowre of earthly blisse, that he might see and know, and yet abstain' (*Areopagitica*). That this view is the right one is suggested by the pattern of the temptations, which is the same as that traditionally imposed on the scriptural accounts of the temptation of Christ in the wilderness. This was the *total* temptation, and the archetype of all subsequent ones. Having rejected the pleasures of the flesh, and of the eyes, and of the pride of life, Christ had nothing more to reject. The scheme, as later diversified, is used by Milton in *Paradise Regain'd*, and by Marvell in the 'Dialogue between the Resolved Soul and Created Pleasure'. Phaedria corresponds to the magic banquet; then Guyon, like Christ, rejects gold, wordly glory, and curious knowledge. In each case the Christian, like Christ, explains that there is a higher reward which he will not throw away by accepting earthly gratifications: the heavenly glory, the true knowledge of God. The proof that the Garden of Proserpina represents the temptation of forbidden knowledge is too complex to set forth here (see 'The Cave of Mammon', in *Elizabethan Poetry*, Stratford-on-Avon Studies, 2, ed. J. R. Brown and Bernard Harris, London, 1960, pp. 151–73). The point to hold on to is, I think, that in this canto Guyon is not being tempted by his own internal concupiscence but by an external enemy, and that in this respect he is sinless in offering his passive resistance, and no more to be accused of seeking the occasion of sin than Christ in the wilderness. His reward is heroic virtue, in the sense given this term by the Church when it adapted it from Aristotle; he has now a habit of good conduct that is a second nature, and that fits him for actions beyond the scope of any ordinarily virtuous man. As the victory over sin in the desert prepared Christ for the victory over death on the Cross, so Guyon's victory over Mammon makes possible the final destruction of the Bower of Bliss. He needs succour after so great an ordeal undergone without supernatural aid; so did Christ, and in either case it was provided by angels. (See the opening of canto viii.) Thus it is a mistake, I think, to interpret Guyon's faint as evidence of his moral weakness. He has, as the eighteenth-century commentator Upton put it, 'gone through a kind of initiation, and passed all the fiery trials; and comes out more temperate and just, as silver tried in the fire'.

In the eighth canto the angel commends Guyon to his Palmer, but it requires Arthur to rescue him from Pyrochles and Cymochles, representing an insubordination of his passions in physical weakness. In the ninth, there is a full-scale allegorical treatment of the House of Alma (the Soul) also called the House of Temperance. This corresponds to the House of Holiness in Book I, and is for the most part very simple allegory, describing the well-ordered human body in terms of a great house. But it is besieged by enemies; and after a canto (x) devoted to a long account of Elizabeth's putative British forebears, Spenser turns to the matter of the siege, and in canto xi writes one of the great passages of the poem, the description of Maleger and his battle with Arthur. Maleger (from Latin *aeger*, sick) is a nightmare figure: 'like a ghost he seem'd, whose grave-clothes were unbound' —a superbly conceived symbol of the ills which attack fallen humanity. The horror of Arthur's combat with this unkillable though apparently lifeless shadow sets it apart from more routine battles, and is another representation of the divine combat with death necessitated by Adam's intemperance.

The final canto, xii, brings Guyon to the climax of his quest, and to the Bower of Bliss. But first he has to get there; and his voyage recapitulates much of the book. He and the Palmer pass Phaedria, for example, and many hidden dangers threatening temperance. At the Bower itself, the human heart that must be cleansed, there are all the spurious beauties that art can provide. The Porter is Genius, but not the Genius of 'life and generation' whom we met in *Epithalamion*; this one, though comely, is antithetical to the good Genius, and 'the foe of life'. Guyon spills his winebowl and breaks his staff. Within there is a false version of the earthly paradise. The fountain, for instance, is not of the law, like that in canto i, but of wantonness; Guyon feels the temptation of its nymphs, but the Palmer corrects him. Then they come within hearing of Acrasia's own music. The rest of the canto and of the book is given in the extract. Acrasia is with her victim in the bower, and the situation is very much the same as the comparable ones in Ariosto and Tasso; Spenser yields little to them in the sweet voluptuousness with which he renders the sensual appeal of Incontinence herself, though in 74 and 75 he actually translates Tasso. The young man her victim is unmanned; like the other victims of this Circe, he is about to be turned into a beast. This is the antithesis of Heroic Virtue. But Acrasia is trapped and Verdant freed; and the whole pleasure palace is destroyed without remorse. The Palmer turns all the beasts back into men; except one, Gryll or Gryllus, who alone of the companions of Ulysses preferred bestiality to manhood, so demonstrating the lowest depths to which incontinence can bring human nature.

Book II is certainly one of the great books, and although it lacks some of the complexity of design of Book I, it takes second place to that inclusive overture.

Canto vii

922. *yblent*: blinded.

924. *firmes*: fixes.

925. *experiment*: practice.

929. Ydle lake: Phaedria's lake, described in canto vi.

933. *yode*: travelled.

934. *reedes*: considers.

940. *uncouth*: strange (with an approach to the modern meaning). *salvage*: savage (but with some of the sense of 'woodlandman' or 'wild man').

944. *seard*: burned.

950. *entayle*: carving.

951. *antickes*: ancient designs.

959. *driven*: smelted.

960. *Ingoes*: ingots.

961. *moniment*: figure.

963. *kesars*: kaisers, emperors.

976. *usuance*: use.

980. *read*: perceive.

981. *still seate*: quiet abode.

983. Mammon: See Matthew vi. 24, and Luke xvi. 13.

988. *Swinck*: labour.

991. *sew*: follow, serve.

993. *mind*: ambition.

1000. *der-doing armes*: feats of high courage.

1001. *honours suit*: the pursuit of honour.

1004. *blend*: defile.

1016. *rowme*: room, place.

1017. *lust*: wish.

1018. *read*: understand.

1020. *reserv'd*: kept, protected.

1034. *brent*: burned.

1039. Adrian: Adriatic.

1044. *upbraid*: utter reproaches.

1050. *empeach*: impair.

1053. *accloyes*: clogs, chokes.

1083. *Ne . . . but*: i.e. for all I know . . .

1088. *mew*: secret place.

1092. *wonne*: dwelling.

1102. *Plutoes . . . raine*: i.e. hell, over which Pluto presided.

1122. Celeno: a Harpy.

1123. *bale*: harm, injury.

1132. *ne . . . ought*: i.e. there was nothing between them.

1161. Stygian: referring to Styx, the infernal river, and thus to hell.

1164. *vaut*: vault. *breaches*: fissures.

1168. Arachne: the spider.

1182. *bends*: bands.

1207. *n'ill*: do not want.

1218. *well he weened*: i.e. he had fully expected.

1219. *assay*: trial.

1221. *Culver*: dove.

1228. *pight*: placed.

1233. *tride*: purified.

1266. *emprise*: enterprise.

1267. *no'te he chuse*: he could not choose.

1268. *mesprise*: scorn.

1281. *stomacke*: resentment.

1282. *portuance*: bearing.

1286. *deface*: put out of countenace.

1300. *Gyeld*: guild-hall. After this encounter Guyon, the temptation of money being finished, embarks on the temptation of false honour in the temple of Philotime.

1308. *preaced*: pressed.

1310. *siege*: seat, throne.

1322. *till . . . fall*: i.e. honour became a base and wordly pursuit.

1325. *gold chaine*: borrowed from Homer, but moralized, this is 'ambition's ladder'.

1331. *sty*: mount.

1351. *hight*: is called.

1352. *wonneth*: dwelleth.

1358. *lust*: wish.

1364. *wote*: know. *unequall*: i.e. not a fit match for hers (ironical).

1366. *other Lady*: as in the previous temptation, Guyon states his preference for the heavenly counterpart of the reward offered. (Guyon now undergoes the temptation to curiosity in the Garden of Proserpina.)

1379. Heben: ebony-tree.

1380. Hellebore: plant supposed to cure madness.

1381. Coloquintida: bitter-apple. Tetra: deadly nightshade.

1382. Samnitis: Savine-tree, used to procure abortions. Cicuta: hemlock.

1384. Socrates. Socrates was put to death by means of a draught of hemlock, but Spenser is wrong in saying he spoke his last philosophy to *Critias*.

1386. *Belamy*: dear friend.

1388. *silver seat*: this detail is probably borrowed from an account of the mystery religions; the seat was on no account to be used.

1399. *but . . . sold*: unless they were supplied from here.

1401. *from . . . daughters*: Referring to Hercules' theft of the apples from the Garden of the Hesperides. The mythological commentators

Spenser knew thought they stood for astronomical knowledge (which was often thought 'curious' or blasphemous).

1404. *Atlanta*: who stopped in the middle of the race to pick up an apple. She had desecrated the shrine of the Great Mother, and was therefore associated with blasphemy.

1406. *Acontius*: He won Cydippe by writing on an apple 'I swear by Artemis that I will marry Acontius'. She picked it up in the precincts of the temple of Artemis, and read the message aloud. This amounted to a solemn oath, and when she refused to keep it the gods intervened against her.

1408. *famous . . . Apple*: Ate, Strife, threw the apple among the assembled gods and goddesses at the wedding of Peleus and Thetis; it was marked 'This should be given to the fairest'. Hence the dispute between Juno, Minerva, and Venus, which was adjudicated by Paris; his presumption in doing so was requited by the Trojan war, a direct consequence of his receiving Helen as a reward from Venus. The goddesses are *Idaean* because the Judgement took place on Mount Ida.

1411. *dempt*: judged.

1412. *meed*: reward.

1421. *Cocytus*: a river in Hades.

1426. *of*: by.

1438. *swinke*: labour.

1439. *drouth*: thirst.

1440. *couth*: knew how to.

1445. *Tantalus*: His torment was regarded by the writers who fitted allegories to ancient myths as a punishment for his profaning the secrets of religion by divulging the table-talk of the gods; or, by revealing the secrets of the mystery-rituals.

1460. *drent*: submerged.

1462. *feculent*: foul (a reference to Pilate's useless washing of his hands).

1470. *Pilate*: punished with Tantalus because of his betrayal of the divinely-sanctioned office of a judge.

1472. *despiteous*: malicious.

1477. *moe*: more.

1486. *doe . . . fall*: cause him fatally to fall.

1500. *three days*: The Christian reference is obvious. Three days was also the period spent in 'hell' by the initiate in mystery-religions.

At this point Guyon has undergone the *total* temptation, on the pattern of Christ's.

Os

Book II, Canto xii, 70–87

1515. *attonce*: together.

1532. *fair Witch*: Acrasia.

1539. *toyes*: amorous play.

1542. *stong*: stung.

1543. *depasturing*: consuming.

1548. *rewd*: pitied.

1561. *earst*: once.

1573. *display*: discover.

1577. *dight to*: prepared for.

1586. *n'ote*: might not.

1591. *thrild*: pierced.

1605. *moniments*: figures, images.

1606. *ras't*: erased.

1611. *blend*: blind, or defile.

1615. *net*: derived from the one used by Vulcan to catch Mars and Venus together.

1616. *formally*: expressly.

1636. *Cabinets*: arbours.

1637. *banket*: banquet. *race*: raze.

1639. *lad*: led.

1655. *aggrate*: please.

1657. *vertuous*: powerful.

Book III. This book, called the Legend of Chastitie, is structurally very different from I and II, but intimately related to—and in some ways continuous with—Book IV. It is not unlikely that parts of it represent earlier work than I and II, and belong to a time when Spenser's principal intention was less to imitate the scope and design of classical epic than to 'overgo Ariosto'. The interweaving stories of Britomart and Arthegall, Marinell and Florimell, Belphoebe and Timias, with many others, given the work an Ariostan quality of lively and complex narrative with many interlocking stories, and most of the themes run through both books. They are separated by six years in dates of publication, but their composition may have been almost consecutive. At some point Spenser decided that he could not allow Scudamour and Amoret to be united at the end of III, and in the 1596 edition he cancelled the last five stanzas of the 1590 text, replacing them by three new ones postponing the union.

It would be unprofitable to attempt a summary of the diverse

narratives of Book III. The important points to grasp at the outset
are that Spenser here celebrates Elizabeth, under the name of Belphoebe,
in her second person 'as a most virtuous and beautifull Lady'; and
that, as we saw in the extract from *Colin Clout* and in *Epithalamion*,
he could include in a treatment of love (for that is what the Legend
of Chastitie amounts to) an exalted poetic philosophy embracing much
more than the relation between the sexes, and glorying in love as the
agent of fertility and order. Thus he can make the Virgin Queen
patroness and exemplar of plenty, fertility, order; Belphoebe, in whom
he invites the Queen to see an image of herself, is the twin sister of
Amoret, whose chastity will express itself in married love.

The cosmic and moral implications of love are present not only in
the stories of Amoret and Belphoebe, but also in those 'Accidents'
of which Spenser speaks in the Letter to Raleigh. An example is 'the
overthrow of Marinell, the misery of Florimell', in this book. The
story of these two persists into Book V. Florimell is based on the
Angelica of Ariosto, similarly pursued and subjected to evil imitation.
Spenser hardly makes it clear what significance she should be given
in the general allegory; but she is a type of the beauty of natural
creation, the opposite yet the complement of the chaotic sea (Marinell)
out of which Love was born. Throughout her life she is pursued for
wicked reasons (by a lustful forester, for instance) and is the victim of
impostures (the Snowy Florimell). Her ultimate union with Marinell
takes place virtually at the end of time, when mutability ceases to reign
in the created world.

Despite the omnipresence of this shadowy allegory, the main purpose
of Book III is accomplished otherwise. In the opening canto Spenser
follows his established procedure: the outgoing knight Guyon meets
the new one, Britomart, maiden warrior defending Chastity (not
simply Virginity), and is overcome by her, since Chastity is a higher
virtue than Temperance. Britomart, because of the different nature of
the book, dominates the narrative to a much lesser degree than Redcross and Guyon in their books, but comes into her own at the end.
Florimell appears; and then, since the first canto contains the key to
the rest, Castle Joyeous. This is the abode of Malecasta, and it is packed
with emblems of unchastity. Britomart arrives and defeats Malecasta's
champions. Cantos ii and iii establish the relationship of Britomart
and Arthegall to Elizabeth and her powers and virtues; iv tells of
Marinell and Florimell; v describes the healing of Timias by Belphoebe
(almost certainly a reference to the quarrel between Raleigh and the

Queen) and ends with Arthur's beautiful apostrophe to Night. Canto
vi is the 'core' canto, in which Spenser exposes the philosophical
heart of his allegory in the myth of the Gardens of Adonis, and eighteen
stanzas of this, the passage in *The Faerie Queene* most famous for the
difficulties of interpretation it presents, form our extract.

First Spenser describes the birth of the twins Belphoebe and Amoret,
daughters of the virgin Chrysogone ('golden-born') by the action of
the sun: 'great Belphoebe' ('virginity') is the older of the two; Amoret
('chaste sexual love') is younger. Venus, leaving her heavenly 'house
of forms' to seek her son Cupid, meets Diana. Together they find
Chrysogone and take one child each, Diana choosing Belphoebe,
'To be upbrought in perfect Maydenhed'. Venus carries Amoret to
her earthly home, the Garden of Adonis. A description of this garden
follows.

Sources for Spenser's philosophy in these lines have been found in
many places, ranging from the exalted speculations of Renaissance
Neo-platonism through Plotinus, one of its ancient sources, to a more
easily available and largely medieval Platonic tradition. The sources
matter only in so far as Spenser's myth is unintelligible without such
information; and in fact only a very little is needed to make it self-
explanatory. The Garden is 'the first seminarie of all things', that is,
the place whence come the seeds—*rationes seminales*, as Augustine
called them—from which all created things develop. It is therefore
under one aspect the *anima mundi*, the Platonic world-soul, providing
the special forms which, when imposed on matter, give all created
things their characteristic shapes and habits. The true Genius, opposite
to the Genius of the Bower of Bliss, and devoted to generation and life,
presides over them, clothes the seminal forms with matter '(sinfull
mire' because the world is fallen and because, in the Platonic scheme,
matter is evil in so far as it is remote from spirit). He sends them out,
and receives them again when, crumbled by time, the seminal
forms return; in due course Chaos (36) will again provide matter for
the re-imposition of the forms, and they will begin a new cycle of
terrestrial life. Though the forms are seen to fade, they constitute eternal
substance by means of this generative cycle.

At 39 the issue, so far fairly simple, grows more complicated.
The presence of Time in the garden, and the description of him as the
enemy of the forms, means that they contain within them the potentia-
lity of their decay when they have taken matter upon them. Not in
themselves eternal, they inhabit a realm between time and eternity.

Generation, and the frank joys of love, have in Time a natural enemy. But without it and its works of mutability there would be no need for generation; its existence depends on the existence of this opponent. In the very heart of the Garden, among flowers suggesting not only pleasure but mortality, is Adonis, the source of forms, and like them between the eternal and the mortal: he is 'subject to mortalitie,/ Yet is eterne in mutabilitie'. The Boar which proved his mortality, is now imprisoned, suggesting that the rule of time and death over creation is but temporary, as Christian believe; we live in the period between the arrival of Death in the world and its ultimate defeat, of which we are assured, and meanwhile the healed Adonis represents the sempiternity of the forms. Thus Spenser adapts not merely the ancient myth, but the religious and philosophical interpretations that attached to it; for Adonis-Thammuz, dying annually and annually reviving, had long been a pagan type of Christ and a symbol of what is 'Eterne in mutabilitie'. The Gardens of Adonis—little pots of flowers that sprang up in a few days and then withered—are equally transformed in Spenser's ambitious allegory into a paradise of love and generation.

With Adonis are Cupid and Psyche, ever since Apuleius an allegory of the soul and its love for God. Psyche, after her trials, joins her divine lover, and their child is Pleasure, the joys of heaven. Milton remembered Spenser's Adonis and his Cupid and Psyche in the Epilogue to *Comus*, where, it must be said, he enriched and improved the allegory. But taking it all together, this passage is, with the Mutability cantos to which it is so closely related, the height of Spenser's achievement as a master of philosophical allegory.

The remainder of the book continues Florimell's story, and introduces other exempla of love. So in vii Satyrane returns to rescue the Squire of Dames, whose plight is a rare instance of Spenser's humour; his task is to find many chaste women. The climax of the book is the rescue of Amoret by Britomart. Amoret is the prisoner of the enchanter Busirane; the meaning is that the love between her and her husband Scudamour is obscured by passion. Scudamour cannot save her; the task falls to Britomart. She observes a Mask of Cupid, illustrating the pains of sensual love; then she lays low Busirane and leaves with Amoret. The flames which had barred Scudamour's entry are now extinct, and Britomart (in the first version) conducts Amoret to a happy reunion with her husband. But in the later version they find him to have disappeared.

III. vi. 26–52

1675. *she*: Diana.

1687. Lucinaes: Juno, in the capacity of patron of women in labour, was called Lucina.

1700. *stead*: place; i.e. lacking Cupid (Amor), she called the baby Amoretta.

1705. Paphos: in Cyprus, the island of Venus. Cytheron: mountain where Venus is said to have been worshipped.

1706. Gnidus: Gnidus, where Venus was worshipped.

1755. *imply*: contain.

1758. *sundry*: separate.

1760. *reasonable souls*: i.e. human beings.

1762. *hew*: forms, shapes.

1776. *when as*: when. *ketch*: catch.

1784. *th'only*: only the.

1798. *flaggy*: drooping.

1807. *no'te*: could she not.

1816. *leman*: mistress.

1822. *Prime*: spring.

1828. This is like Eden in many accounts, including Milton's.

1841. *entrayld*: entwined.

1892. *Caprifole*: honeysuckle.

1844. *throng*: press.

1848. Hyacinthus: killed while playing quoits with Apollo, who made the flower that sprang from his blood an emblem of his mourning.

1850. Narcisse: Narcissus, who died of self-love, and was transformed into a flower.

1851. Amaranthus: from the flower so called because it does not fade. There is no myth of Amaranthus.

1853. Amintas: conventional shepherd's name in pastoral; here Sir Philip Sidney.

1860. *skill*: knowledge.

1864. *sooth*: truth.

1871. *Father* . . . : Adonis is made to represent the 'substance' of stanzas 37–8.

1876. *cloyd*: gored.

1881. *losen*: loose.

1884. *haunt*: sojourn, dwell, visit.

1893. *upbrayes*: reproaches.

1898. *aggrate*: please, gratify.
1910. *Paragone*: model of excellence.
1917. *launched*: lanced, pierced.

Book IV. Possibly Spenser discovered, in writing the fourth book, that he could not maintain the Ariostan impetus, and that more schematic allegory suited his gifts better. At any rate, Book IV, is the weakest of the six, though it is so closely related to Book III, one of the best. The Legend of Friendship has as its heroes the friends Cambel and Triamond, whose story Spenser borrowed from Chaucer's unfinished *Squire's Tale*. But the story is diversified so as to provide different exempla of love and friendship; and characters from other books—Guyon and Braggadocchio, Britomart and Arthegall, Satryane, Scudamour, Florimell and Archimago, appear from time to time. There are five main stories. Spenser's self-denial in cancelling the original conclusion of III is rewarded by the opportunity to describe, in a justly famous passage of canto v, Scudamour's sojourn in the House of Care. In the sixth canto Britomart and Arthegall fall in love; upon their union depends not only the future happiness of Britain but much of Spenser's fifth Book. In vii Belphoebe saves Amoret from the attentions of a lawless salvage man; as Spenser puts it in the following canto:

> . . . beautie, which was made to represent
> The great Creatours owne resemblance bright,
> Unto abuse of lawlesse lust was lent,
> And made the baite of bestiall delight.

In this fallen world, 'the band of vertuous mind', or the love of friends, is nobler than the love of family or of women. Yet all these loves grow on the same stem; and the core of Book IV is really Scudamour's account of how he won Amoret. He forces admission into the Temple of Venus, past Doubt and Delay and Danger (the unapproachability of virtuous women), until he comes upon a paradise of good pleasure, described in the extract. In this place of innocence he finds many famous friends. Finally he reaches the Temple. Concord reconciles the extreme passions of love and hate, and maintains the world in balance. The goddess herself is Hermaphrodite, symbolizing the union in love of man and woman (Spenser had used the same figure for Amoret and Scudamour in the cancelled stanzas of III). The prayer of the lover to Venus is based on the address of Lucretius to Venus in the *De Rerum Natura*; this is *alma Venus*, *Venus genetrix*, giver of pleasure and generation throughout creation. 'So all the world by thee at first was made.' Scudamour echoes this adoration of the 'queene of th'ayre,/Mother of laughter, and welspring of bliss.' Then he perceives about her the proper qualities of the beloved: Womanhood, Shamefastness, and the rest. In the lap of Womanhood he sees Amoret. The goddess smiles on him, and he leads Amoret away. How characteristic this allegory is of Spenser should be clear to readers who have studied *Colin Clout*, *Epithalamion*, and *Faerie Queene* III. The blend of open delight in sexual love with a respect for the proper prohibitions is further illustrated by the intervention of Busirane in what seems a perfect love; for the enchanter came between Scudamour and his bride on their wedding night, and in the altered version Scudamour is still at this point deprived of his wife. In fact Book IV ends without his recovering her.

The main business of the concluding cantos is the bringing together of Marinell and Florimell. Canto xi is a large set-piece, perhaps something Spenser had by him, concerning the marriage of the Thames and the Medway; it fits the resolution of discord into concord, and the prospective union of Marinell and Florimell, but it somewhat emphasizes the looseness of this, perhaps the least attractive book in the poem. This is, admittedly, a matter of appearance. Mr. Fowler, after studying the numerology of the poem, claims that 'the fourth is in many ways the most unified of all the books of the *Faerie Queene*'.

IV. x. 23–52

1918. This 'paradise' should be compared with the good paradise of generation in III. vi, and with the evil paradise of II. xii.

1922. *blesse*: bliss.

1932. *disloigned*: removed.

1940. *shankes*: legs.

1944. *balkt*: quibbled.

1954. Hylas: a youth beloved of Hercules.

1956. Pirithous: the friend who descended with Theseus into hell.

1957. Pylades: his friendship with Orestes was famous from the time of Euripides.

1958. Titus: The story of Titus and Giseppus in the *Decameron* of Boccaccio (10th Day) tells how Titus accused himself of a murder for which Giseppus had accepted responsibility.

1959. Damon: stood as hostage for Pythias when he was under sentence of death.

1981. *Temple of* Diane: see Acts, xix.

1986. *that which . . . framed*: the temple at Jerusalem.

1987. *see*: abode.

1994. *semblant*: appearance.

1996. *Danisk*: Danish.

1998. *raught*: reached.

2017. *reed*: speech.

2031. *quight*: deal with.

2041. *uneath*: with difficulty.

2042. *empeach*: hinder.

2060. *hight*: allocated.

2065. *durefull*: lasting.

2070. *brickle*: brittle.

2074. Phidias: the great Athenian sculptor; Spenser is probably thinking, however, of the statue by Praxiteles at Cnidos, with which a young man fell in love.

2093. *toyes*: sports.

2099. *sorts*: companies.

2101. *some . . . disdayning*: i.e. some of the disdain of a mistress.

2116. *dædale*: intricately built, as if by Daedalus the greater artificer.

2159. *guyse*: fashion.

2163. *desse*: dais.

2175. *submisse*: submissive.

2179. *rate*: manner.

Book V. In this book Spenser returns to a scheme resembling those of Books I and II, and his examination of the virtue of Justice is perhaps the most schematic of all. His allusions to contemporary affairs are both more persistent and more germane to the whole argument than in any other book save the first.

The Book opens with an eleven-stanza prologue lamenting the change that has come over the world since the Golden Age; Astraea, goddess of Justice, whose presence symbolized the order and justice of the first days, has departed, and the present age is an age of stone. Not only the affairs of men, but the whole order of the world—indeed the very movement of the planets—have grown hopelessly irregular. Justice, the 'most sacred' of the virtues, proceeds now from great

Princes, as from Elizabeth, 'that doest highest sit/In seate of iudgement, in th'Almighties stead.'

The action of the book is supposed to take place after the departure of Astraea, when the administration of Justice was in such hands as those of Bacchus and Hercules and Spenser's Knight of Justice, Arthegall—so named from Arthgalle, a mythical king of Britain; Spenser probably liked the name because it could mean 'equal to Arthur'. Arthegall, by his union with Britomart, was to establish, as Arthur did, the line of British kings stretching to the Tudors. Primarily he represents pure Justice; he exactly enforces the law, with the aid of the iron man Talus and his flail—a sort of police force without the right to initiate legal action, which simply carries out the decision of the justice. The ultimate quest of Arthegall, whom Astraea has educated for the purpose, is the destruction of Grantorto (Injustice) and the release of Irena (meaning, probably, both 'peace' and 'Ireland'). The opening canto contains the quest in little, on the pattern of Book I; for Sangliere is forced in justice to carry the head of the lady he has killed. Next Arthegall and Talus suppress Pollente and Munera, who represents the buying and selling of justice (perhaps with some glances at specific contemporary cases of such venality) and then deal with a mad enemy of the social order, the Giant who proposes communism of the sort advocated by the sect of Anabaptists. Arthegall explains to him that he cannot eliminate inequality, level the mountains and the social ranks. At this discomfiture the people, disappointed of their gains, grow mutinous and have to be subdued by Talus. In his contempt for the democratic or communist programme of the Giant, which he regarded as contrary to law both natural and divine, Spenser is merely expressing the well-established views of the age; justice depends upon a divinely ordered inequality in the creation.

The third canto interpolates the marriage of Florimell and the final exposure of Braggadocchio, neatly reserved for this legend of Justice. Illuminating Aristotle's division of justice, the fourth gives instances of distributive (as opposed to corrective) justice, and brings Arthegall into conflict with Radigund. All Renaissance epic heroes have something in common with Hercules, and Arthegall here reflects him in his weakness, when he became the effeminate slave of Iole and Omphale. He falls under the 'monstrous regiment of women', the tyranny of a woman who has 'skane off the samefast band,/With which wise Nature did them strongly bynd,/T 'obay the heasts of mans well ruling hand.' This unnatural situation—the woman as ruler over the man—is excusable only when it comes about not through a seeking after 'licentious libertie' but because the heavens themselves have lifted a woman 'to lawfull soveraintie' (v. 25). This necessary exception should not be imputed to a prudent inconsistency on Spenser's part; it was, again, a fairly standard view. The news of Arthegall's enslavement having reached Britomart by Talus, she sets out to rescue him, eluding Guile on the way, and stopping at Isis Church for spiritual support.

As in earlier books, we have one of the really important, if somewhat mysterious, passages in canto vii. The Isis allegory is brief but central, and is entirely contained in the extract, stanzas 1–23. To undertsand what Spenser is about one needs to know something of contemporary views on the relation of Justice to Equity. Spenser in the Church of Isis makes his version of what was known as a *Templum Iustitiae*. The tradition goes back to Augustan Rome, and in later Roman law the judges were called priests of Justice, so that Spenser's strange priests may be thought of as such. But he has announced that what he will 'treat here presently' is 'That part of Iustice, which is Equity.' Now some Roman jurists could claim that Equity is the source of Justice, or even that, properly conceived, the two are identical. Without Equity there is no Justice. Equity is of heavenly origin; as Portia remembered, it will not, like law, 'spill the principal to save the part'. It would always prefer to save rather than to spill.

Roman law was not received in England, though there was considerable interest in the subject during Tudor times—and since Elizabeth represented herself as Empress, some parts of Roman law adhered to her imperial propaganda. The English maxim, however, is 'equity follows law'; it is obviously not the fount of law. Under Elizabeth it was, accordingly, a subject of much dispute and speculation. The courts of equity which derived their authority from the royal prerogative, and which were independent of the common law courts, grew greatly in importance. The most notable were the Courts of Chancery and Star Chamber. Chancery dealt in civil cases and was bound by no precedent, operating as 'the conscience of the Queen', as represented by her Lord Chancellor. Star Chamber was a development of her Council, and dealt with criminal causes, such as scandals and seditions touching the security of the monarch, and also with recusancy. Both were equity courts. Chancery could remedy injustices that found no remedy in common law: for example, breaches of trust, or the complaint of a poor man wronged by a powerful nobleman, who could pack the jury in a lower court. Common lawyers of the time much resented the growth of the power of Chancery, and it was certainly associated with claims to absolute monarchic power—the very claims embodied in the imperial myth expressed by Spenser in Book I. Star Chamber was hated by recusants, and notorious for the severity of its punishments. Parliament abolished it in 1641, as soon as it had the power.

With these points in mind, let us look at Spenser's *Templum Iustitiae*. He borrows from Plutarch the myth of Isis and Osiris, freely adapting it to his needs. Isis was identified with Justice, and with Astraea, and with substance, as Spenser describes it in III. vi; Justice gives perishable forms to the substance of Equity. Osiris is justice as administered, without benefit of equity, in the courts of the common law. The priests are jurists; their abstinence from wine, earlier described as the blood of the rebel Titans, stands for their implacable opposition to riot and recusancy. The foot on the crocodile and the wand signify the control of justice by equity in both criminal and civil causes (as in Star Chamber and Chancery). The crocodile, then, is law-without-equity, such as Arthegall, incapable alone of the exercise of imperial equity, has practised.

The dream of Britomart changes her from priest to empress, robed in imperial purple and crowned with the sun; she is the progenitress of Elizabeth. The tempest and fire are rebellions against her power, suppressed by the crocodile, or the law of England. The presumption of the crocodile after this may represent the impatience of the common lawyers with the claims of the prerogative courts; more generally, Justice impatient of Equity. The union of Britomart and the crocodile is the full union of Justice and Equity in the imperial power of the queen. The priestly interpreter explains that the crocodile is Arthegall, justice-without-equity; his union with equity completes the imperial justice of Elizabeth, and the Isis allegory allies this to the function of love in ordering and maintaining the frame of the whole world. (For a fuller exposition, see *Bulletin of the John Rylands Library*, 47, Sept. 1964.)

The Church of Isis, then, has the same degree of allegorical complexity as some passages in Book I, and is further evidence of Spenser's power to give a poet's attention to a grand philosophical design without losing his peculiarly close relationship to the imperial moment in which, as he saw it, he lived. Fortified by this prediction of her power to right wrongs, Britomart defeats Radigund, equitably repeals the unnatural 'liberty of women', and releases Arthegall. They proceed to accomplish various tasks, in which ethical more and more yields place to political allegory. The eighth canto treats of the war with Spain, with the Soudan as the King of Spain and his wife Adicia (Greek 'injustice') as the injustice to which he is wedded. Transparently this canto describes the defeat of the Armada, and other historical matters. In the ninth canto the main business is again historical. After a passage relating to Lord Grey's campaign against the wild Irish, Spenser deals, in the passage describing Mercilla's refusal to pardon the crimes of Duessa, with Elizabeth's condemnation of Mary Queen of Scots. But as the passage here given (27–50) demonstrates, there is much more than this single event in Spenser's mind.

Mercilla is Isis under another aspect, and in her presence we are again in the English prerogative courts, where people seek what the common law denied them, a justice unperverted by 'brybes, or threates'. The poet so severely punished had accused the Queen of 'forged guile', words which in the Isis canto are associated with the rebellious Typhon-crocodile. His offence and its punishment alike remind us of Star Chamber. Mercilla's throne is a reminder that the Queen's State was symbolically present in Star Chamber, a prerogative court. Above it is a cloud-like canopy, reminiscent of a pictorial *maestà*. The two swords are the sceptre of clemency and the sword of justice. Equity is not indiscriminate forgiveness. Around Mercilla are the Litae, whose function is Equity. The lion at her feet fulfils Britomart's dream, and is the common law of England in bondage to imperial Equity. From this presence Arthur goes forth on the immediate business of the empress, which is the Netherlands campaign against the Spanish supporters of the papal antichrist. The eleventh canto presses the defeat of the Spanish rather beyond any point it was to reach. Arthur hears from Belge an account of the temple of Geryon; he visits the Temple, and kills the fiendish beast that lurks under the altar. This Temple of Injustice is designed as the antithesis of the Temple of Isis.

Spenser then turns to Arthegall and the fulfilment of his quest, the liberation of Irena from Grantorto. On the way he meets Burbon, who is Henri IV; when he throws away the shield given him by Redcross Henri is embracing the Catholic religion, which he did in 1593 as 'the price of Paris', greatly to the distress of Elizabeth. Arthegall here probably represents Essex, a supporter of Henri IV; and in giving Talus so large a part in his victory over remaining dissident elements in France, Spenser is again exaggerating the English contribution. Arthegall now reaches the climax of his quest. In rescuing Irena he probably represents both the activities of Grey, of which Spenser had first-hand knowledge, and the militant policies of Essex, though he was not to fight in Ireland till 1599. Arthegall kills the tyrant Grantorto and restores Irena to her throne; but on his way home he is assailed by Envy and Detraction and the Blatant Beast—now to be an important character in the poem; these are allusions to the ill-repute that came upon Grey on his return from Ireland.

The fifth book is markedly inferior to I and II. Towards the end the contemporary allusions intrude to the point where the grander allegorical design is obscured. But although Spenser seems to have lost some of the extraordinary flexibility and inclusiveness of Book I, there is a particular fineness of imaginative design in the triple portraits of Isis, Mercilla, and Grantorto at the trial; they are like three spatially related though separate parts in a great fresco.

V. vii. 1–23

2214. Talus is not admitted because Equity thinks it 'better to reforme then to cut off the ill'.

2219. *long locks*: this detail Spenser borrowed from an account of the priesthood of Rhea; otherwise the priests derive from Plutarch's *Isis and Osiris*.

2253. *desining*: indicating.

2257. *house of Iove*: sky.

2272. *Gyants*: Throughout the book, symbols of lawlessness and rebellion; Plutarch says that vines sprang from the blood of these Titans when they failed to defeat the gods and were thrown to earth, so that wine is their rebellious blood.

2273. *Phlegrean*: the battle took place at Phlegra near Naples; the plain has many volcanic cones.

2276. *her sonnes*: the Titans were sons of Gea, the Earth.

2317. *stowre*: disturbance.

2336. *melancholy*: (stress the second syllable).

2348. *apayd*: satisfied.

2366. *adawed*: terrified.

V. ix. 27–50

2399. *sheene*: fair.

2410. *plights*: folds.

2426. *Maugre*: despite.

2435. Litae: 'prayers'; but Spenser is thinking of the *horai*, called by Hesiod Eunomia (Good Government), Dike (Justice) and Eirene (Peace). Spenser adds, with typical syncretism, Temperance and Reverence.

2436. *Themis*: Goddess personifying Justice.

2457. *royne*: rear. *redound*: overflow.

2462. *boone*: favour (they ask to be given some adventure or quest). *mought*: could.

2464. *stoupe*: concession.

2470. *adaw*: subdue.

2474. *doe*: make.

2475. *entertake*: entertain.

2479. *indifferent*: impartial.

2487. *eftsoones*: forthwith.

2489. *witness forth*: bear witness to (the justice of the proceedings).

2498. *condition*: quality, behaviour.

2506. *To all assayes*: on every occasion.

2507. *appele*: accuse.

2508. *enured*: committed.

2523. These characters appeared in Books III and IV.

2527. *aspyred*: i.e. aspired to.

2528. *deryve*: obtain.

2533. *proofe*: effect.

2537. *untitled*: Mary Queen of Scots abdicated in 1567.

2539. *fact*: crime.

2546. *The* Kingdomes care: Lord Burleigh.

2554. *Commons sute*: The Commons twice petitioned the Queen to put Mary to death.

2562. *forren powre*: To execute Mary was to offend Scotland, France, and Spain; and the Armada was a direct consequence of Elizabeth's act.

2578. Ate: Strife.

2581. *appeach*: accuse.

2583. *traynes*: plots.

2586. *detect*: accuse.

2601. *thrall*: prisoner.

2602. This reflects Elizabeth's real perturbation and her reluctance to sign Mary's death warrant.

Book VI. In this book the knight of Courtesy, Calidore, accomplishes his quest of the Blatant Beast. It is in some ways similar to I, II, and V in its design—Calidore meets Arthegall in the first canto, and the first has the seeds of the rest. After encountering various exempla of courtesy and discourtesy, Calidore falls into a 'pastoral truancy' in mid-course, somewhat on the analogy of Red Cross. But the tone of the work is different from anything that has gone before, and the deep allegories of the 'core' cantos in the earlier books, with all their involution and extravagance, are lacking here. Instead, Spenser does something different, in the apparition of the Graces to Colin Clout in the passage here extracted.

We cannot understand Spenser's 'courtesy' by thinking of the word in its attenuated modern meaning. In his Prologue he distinguishes between the merely outward agreeableness of manner that can pass in a fallen age for this virtue, and the real thing, which 'brancheth forth in brave nobilitie,/And spreds it selfe through all civilitie.' Courtesy is the manner of behaving of a gentleman or nobleman, and in a sense is the virtue that such poems as Spenser's were meant to inculcate: 'to fashion a gentleman or noble person in vertuous and gentle discipline', as he himself puts it in the Letter to Raleigh. Courtesy belongs, then, to the noble (the *non vile*) and not to the base-born. There was much dispute about this, and from Dante forward the orthodox view was that a man was ennobled by his deeds, and not by his birth; but in Spenser, as in the final plays of Shakespeare, noble birth is a prerequisite of courtesy, and even courteous savages turn out to be noble. Of course not all the nobly born are courteous; there are cases in which the grafting of civility on to nature has not taken, as it sometimes does not when a gardener matches a cultivated scion with a base stock.

Courtesy, in the broad sense of 'civility', the sense of *noblesse oblige*, the true gentleness which makes for decency and honour in civil and military life—this courtesy was a virtue in which Spenser's time took an acute interest. There were in Italy and in France and in England many 'courtesy-books', of which the most famous was and is Castiglione's *Courtier*. Their object was to provide the proper discipline for a courtier—to fashion a gentleman by precept, example and philosophical justification. Spenser's sixth book translates such precepts and philosophies into romance narrative; here more than anywhere else he approaches the mood of the Greek novella *Daphnis and Chloe*, and doubtless remembered also not only the courtesy of Sidney himself but the philosophy embodied in the romance-narrative of his prose-epic *Arcadia*. The tradition proved fruitful: nowhere is the admiration of Shakespeare for Spenser more clearly illustrated than in his final plays, which are often very close in tone to *Faerie Queene VI*.

The object of Calidore, Spenser's knight of Courtesy, is to subdue slander and evil speaking at its source, but also to demonstrate the gentleness of the gentleman: to be mild when strength is out of place, to champion women, show politeness to inferiors, and to oppose instances of discourtesy wherever they occur. In the course of the book they occur with some frequency. The overthrow of discourtesy in the opening canto involves a curious tale of a bridge of beards, where Calidore chastises a churl for cutting off men's beards and women's hair, and mercifully right the wrongs of a lady who had opposed him. The second canto introduces Childe Tristram, victor over a wicked and discourteous knight, who, though apparently merely a wild young man of the forest (like the sons of Cymbeline in Shakespeare's play), is of royal birth, as Calidore recognizes from his appearance. Then he tends a wounded knight, another obligation of courtesy. His lady Priscilla, who has risked her father's anger by being caught in a compromising position with her lover, Calidore takes home; and by a knightly equivocation contrives to keep her out of trouble. The implication is that the courteous man will prevaricate to save a reputation. A little later he himself stumbles on a secluded pair of lovers, and manages to convince them of the innocence of his intentions; but Serena, the lady, wanders away to gather flowers, and is carried off by the Blatant Beast. Calidore saves her, and pursues the beast, leaving her to her lover Calepine. He takes her to the castle of Sir Turpine, a discourteous knight, who refuses them admittance. Turpine and Calepine fight, and Calepine is saved by a 'salvage man'—another 'natural' who turns out to be of the noble birth necessary to courtesy. This savage cures Calepine's wounds, and entertains the lovers in the forest. Calepine gets lost, and Serena sets out to travel with the savage. They meet Arthur and Timias (Raleigh), who is himself smarting under slanders (an allusion to Raleigh's disgrace when he married Elizabeth Throckmorton). Serena and Timias stay with a Hermit, while Arthur and the Salvage Man go on. The Hermit cures Timias and Serena of the wounds inflicted by evil speaking—not by ointments, but by psychological advice. Arthur and the Salvage Man defeat Turpine, but allow him and Blandina to live on in their falseness and treachery; after another treacherous attack, Arthur has no more mercy and hangs Turpine by his heels from a tree. Meanwhile Timias and Serena meet Mirabella, who is undergoing a grotesque punishment for discourteous treatment of her lovers. Timias is captured by Disdain, and Serena flees. Arthur

Ps

frees Timias and Mirabella goes on her way, expiating her uncourtly
disdain. Calepine turns up just in time to save Serena from a band of
cannibals who are admiring her naked body as a prelude to eating
it (this is one of the most sensual passages in the poem: the prurience
of the savages represents, to use C. S. Lewis's words, the sexual
nature in disease, a highly developed lust which is one of courtesy's
enemies).

After a long interval, Spenser returns to Calidore, who has been
in pursuit of the Beast. But now begins his 'truancy', his sojourn in
the idyllic pastoral retreat of Pastorella and her supposed father Meliboee. He settles happily in the house of Meliboee, and lives the life
of pastoral content, described by Meliboee in lines (ix. 20–21) which
may well have been in Shakespeare's mind when he produced his
light-hearted but rigorous examination of the pastoral genre (so
popular at the time) in *As You Like It*. Meliboee's attack on gardens
(emblems of the interference of art in the innocent life of nature) looks
forward to Marvell's sophisticated handling of the same theme in
'The Mower against Gardens'. Calidore embraces this life, and
remembers, when a shepherd swain of Pastorella's grows jealous, to
treat his inferior rival with courtesy. Pastorella begins to love
Calidore; but at the beginning Spenser reminds us that the knight's
time is not his own, and that he should not be 'Unmyndfull of his vow
and high beheast'. Nevertheless, it is in the midst of this premature
pastoral retirement that he is blessed with the vision of the maidens
dancing around the three Graces to the music of Colin Clout. This
encounter is the subject of our only extract from Book VI.

The reader might care to refer Spenser's Graces to the many repre-
sentations of them in Renaissance painting, and particularly to Botticelli's version in the *Primavera*. There are many ancient precedents for
showing them in a group, though not invariably with only one facing
the spectator; nor are they always naked. For an account of the relation
between Spenser's Graces and the tradition, which grew extremely
complicated in the sixteenth century, see Edgar Wind's *Pagan Mysteries
in the Renaissance* (London, 1958), pp. 33 ff. Here they represent the
civil delight which good love spreads through human society (they
are often so associated with Venus) and are the opposites of the slan-
derous and dis-graceful trio mentioned earlier in the Canto: Despetto,
Decetto and Defetto, Contempt, Deceit, and Detraction. In the midst
of them Spenser, in a rare autobiographical interlude all the more
remarkable for coming at the crucial point of a book in his epic, places

his own love, and Colin Clout represents himself as singing her praises, broken off, as it were, by the innocent intervention of Calidore. So, Spenser seems to say, his labours on his huge poem were interrupted by the events described in the *Amoretti* and the *Epithalamion*; he himself has been guilty of a pastoral truancy; and in 28 he asks pardon of the Queen for introducing a passage in a praise of her 'poore handmayd', for he had after all spent his life celebrating her greater glory. Some feel that the lady celebrated as a 'country lass', and made equal to the Graces, is not Elizabeth Boyle but the Rosalind of *Shepheardes Calender* and *Colin Clout*. This seems unlikely; the praise here offered her, as mediator of virtue and delight through love is close to the tone of *Epithalamion*.

There follows an emergency in which Calidore's courage, and the cowardice of his rival, confirm Pastorella in her love; but the end of the pastoral paradise is at hand, for brigands attack it and carry off Pastorella, Meliboee, and others. The brigands fight with slavers, and all their prisoners are killed except Pastorella and one other; Calidore eventually rescues her from under a heap of bodies. He does what he can to restore the pastoral community, and rides off with Pastorella. The courtesy of innocence, Calidore learns, is all too vulnerable; in a wicked world the best that can be had is a courtesy constantly defended by men of chivalry. By means of a birthmark (for this is like a story in the Arcadia, or the plot of a lost late play of Shakespeare's) Pastorella is restored to her noble parents. Calidore captures the Blatant Beast; but it escapes:

> Thenceforth more mischiefe and more scath he wrought
> To mortal men then he had done before;

indeed, he has lately, says Spenser, grown stronger and more out-rageous, and spares not even the rhymes of poets. On this note he ends the book, and, except for the fragment of Book VII, the poem. The 'Argument' of this last canto speaks of Calidore binding the beast, not of his having escaped; but whatever Spenser's motives in adding the last four stanzas—and they may be little more than his common complaint that poetry was often, in these fallen times, subject to detraction and neglect—it is clear that the decision to leave the enemy of Courtesy at large is of a piece with his usual practice. The victory of Redcross prefigures, but does not bring about, the end of the world; Guyon's victory is incomplete. Spenser found in the life of his own times, to quote a modern poet, an 'image of time's end'; but he saw in them also the evidence of mutability and the decay of the world, when times grew worse and men with them. The knight's courtesy reflects, and his courage protects, the virtues of the 'antique time'; but he must be unflagging, for the enemies of virtue are unsleeping. So the great poem ends consistently, despite its incompleteness. At the heart of it is the tension between time and eternity, evil and good; and Spenser was too much alive, too much aware of the significant acts of his own contemporaries, to pretend a final resolution in time. The best a true poem could offer was shadows of the promised end.

VI. x. 10–28

2633. *in compasse*: around. *stemme*: encircle.

2636. *enchaced*: set.

2638–46. This refers primarily to the constellation. The battle between the Centaurs and the Lapiths took place not at the wedding of Theseus and Ariadne but at the wedding of Pirithous and Hippodamia.

2662. *paravaunt*: in front.

2665. *jolly*: fine, gay.

2666. *rout*: company.

2668. *Colin Clout*: i.e. Spenser.

2671. *lout*: bow.

2676. *spright*: spirit.

2704. *in place*: i.e. back again.

2710. *dilate*: enlarge upon, explain.

2713. *fee*: service.

2720. Eurynome: daughter of Ocean and mother of the Graces.

2723. Æacidee: Peleus, son of Aeacus.

2727. *cherry*: cherish.

2732. *semblaunt*: demeanour.

2735. *demeane*: conduct.

2743. *froward*: turned away.

2744. *afore*: facing forward.

2747. *traced*: danced.

2750. *enraced*: implanted.

2755. *daughter . . . day*: The star Venus (evening star).

2759. *beseemes*: becomes.

2766. *meane*: average. *degree*: rank.

2767. *resemblaunce*: appearance.

2768. *dare*: i.e. dare assault.

2772. *apace*: copiously.

2778. *minime*: musical note (short song).

Two Cantos of Mutability. This fragment was added to the 1609 edition of *The Faerie Queene*. The full title provided by the publisher is *Two Cantos of Mutabilitie; which, both for forme and matter, appeare to be parcell of some following booke of the Faerie Queene, under the Legend of Constancie.* The cantos are labelled vi and vii, and there are also two stanzas of viii. That they belong to *Faerie Queene* has been disputed, but it appears more than likely that they were written for 'some part' of the poem; the publisher's belief was doubtless founded on the division into cantos, the use of the Irish Arlo as elsewhere in the poem, and the content of VII. vi. 37; of course he may have had other proof. There is no reason to believe that Spenser wrote his books in order from first to last stanza, and he may well have written a 'core' canto of philosophical allegory such as the Garden of Adonis passage before he illustrated its theme in the rest of the book; a point well made by C. S. Lewis in *The Allegory of Love*, pp. 353 ff. These cantos are perhaps all that remains of a projected book, the contents of which we, of course, cannot even guess at. It may not have been Book VII, and the publisher's 'Legend of Constancie' may be no more than a good guess—the name of the virtue is antithetical to Mutability. Mr. Alastair Fowler has now produced strong numerological reasons for believing that the fragment is indeed of Book VII, and that the legend was of Constancy (p. 227, &c.). Much dispute has centred on the question of when Spenser wrote these cantos, and some have even held them to be early and rejected drafts; an incomprehensible view, surely, of what many take to be Spenser's finest verse, and one of the great philosophical poems of the language. In any case, their survival is very fortunate. The incomplete state of *Faerie Queene* makes insoluble many problems concerning the full interpretation of what is extant; but these cantos are valuable not only in themselves but also for the way they illuminate their predecessors and confirm us in our understanding, however partial, of Spenser's mind.

The extract here given includes the whole of canto vii except for the two prefatory stanzas and stanzas 28–46, which are described below. The fragmentary eighth canto consists of the two stanzas here reprinted. Canto vi proposes the topic of Change, and calls Mutability herself a daughter of the Titans (charged in Book V, it will be recalled, with the guilt of having brought rebellion and intemperance into the order of the world). Mutability has altered the original good order of the creation, defaced Nature and Justice, and brought in death for life. She is, in fact, under one aspect, the disaster that came upon the sublunary world with the fall of Adam. Now she aspires to the empire of heaven, beyond that part of the world admittedly given over to time and change. First she claims the moon, whose sphere is the border between the two worlds. The sign of this is an eclipse, causing terror among men at this hint that Chaos is resuming its ancient reign. But Mercury investigates, and reports to Jove, who tells the heavenly powers that a daughter of the Titans—'Earths cursed seed'—is once again challenging heaven. Mutability, pressing on with her presumptuous task, arrives at the council, and states her claim. The Gods admire her beauty, and Jupiter, though he reproaches her pride, is disarmed by it. He explains his pre-eminence, and tells the 'foolish gerle' to 'ceasse' her 'idle claime'. Mutability denies that he can judge it impartially, and appeals to 'the God of Nature'. A hearing is appointed, to be held on Arlo-Hill in Ireland.

Spenser now inserts a myth, based on the *Metamorphoses* of Ovid, to explain why this beautiful place (also used in the previous book as the dancing-place of the Graces) has lost some of its original beauty and innocence; the foolish Faunus contrived on this hill to see Diana bathing naked. The punishment was to be hunted as Actaeon was; and Diana abandoned the hill, its forest and stream to wolves and thieves. The purpose of this elaborate mythological intrusion is to stress the part played by human curiosity—the concupiscence of the eye—in the fall of nature and the establishment of the reign of Mutability.

Canto vii describes the hearing before Nature. All creatures attend, and are marshalled by 'Natures Sergeant', Order. Nature—neither man nor woman, unsearchable by any eye—takes her place in a pavilion. Flowers spring beneath her feet, the trees bud and break into leaf. She is 'Still mooving, yet unmoved from her sted' (and so contains in herself the secret answer to Mutability, who is only movement, and does not understand its relation to stillness, or Time's to Eternity). Mutability makes her plea to 'the equall (impartial) mother'. She claims her Titan heritage, argues that the Earth is her thrall; everything there flourishes only to decay, human life is dominated by change. The ocean moves continually, and the fish in it; the other elements are subject to alteration. She then calls forth a procession of times and seasons to prove her point. First come the seasons, then the months (beginning this time with March), then Day and Night, the Hours, and Life and Death. All these are sumptuously characterized, and their indisputable evidence of change plentifully stressed. Jove replies, claiming power over Time, whose ravages are the essence of Mutability's plea; but she returns to the attack, arguing that even the heavenly bodies alter: the moon changes, the planets seem to wander from their courses; and this makes them her subjects. Nothing, she concludes triumphantly, nothing in the whole universe escapes her authority. Nature's judgement is brief and gnomic: she (or he) allows that all things are mutable; but holds that change is the medium whereby each thing maintains and perfects itself, so that it is servant and not master. Mutability seems to be seeking her own alteration and decay; and truly the time will come, at the end of time, when there will be no more change. The eighth canto in its first stanza comments upon the truth of Mutability's assertions of decay; but the second reflects on Nature's reply, that time and movement will cease, and all rest eternally in God at the great Sabbath, for which he prays.

The full weight of these cantos depends upon Spenser's skill in converting into mythological narrative both a considerable body of traditional philosophical explanation and—which is more important for the modern reader—the basic patterns of his own imagination. Scholars, studying the sources of the cantos with a view to making their meaning plain, have discovered a wide variety of analogues in poetry and philosophy—in Ovid and Lucretius, in the neoplatonic philosophy of Plotinus, in the speculations of Boethius, mainstay of medieval philosophy, and even in the thought of the contemporary philosopher Giordano Bruno, who stayed for a time in Oxford and London before he was condemned by the Inquisition. For the most part these erudite inquiries confirm one's sense that Spenser was dependent upon no one particular source, but on well-established philosophical ideas which appear in various forms throughout the history of philosophy, and especially in those parts of it most valued by his contemporaries. Nevertheless, any student who can come by the summaries in the relevant volume of the Variorum edition is urged to do so, as they contain many more insights into Spenser's meaning than could be included in this brief discussion.

Ovid was clearly in his mind, and not only as a model for pleasant metamorphoses. As Mr. Nelson (see Bibliography) observes, Spenser, like any Renaissance poet, chose his models advisedly, and Ovid's long poem is 'the classical work on the subject of Mutability'. From it Spenser borrowed his Nature (though he has other sources in a long medieval tradition) and also the three strands of narrative: Mutability's challenge, the story of Faunus, and the pageant of the times and seasons.

Ovid too speaks of a golden time, before the Titans rebelled; and Spenser remembers his account of their rebellion in *Metamorphoses*. We should remember that Ovid had by no means lost his medieval reputation as a sage providing pagan 'shadows' of true doctrine, and the last book of his poem, in a passage from which the Renaissance derived valued knowledge of that lost philosopher, quotes Pythagoras at length on change and related topics.

But Spenser is never really classical, nor a close imitator of the classical; and there is a familiarly medieval tone in this allegory too. He himself points to Chaucer's *Parlement of Fowles* as the source of the judicial court of Nature, and refers us back to Alanus de Insulis, a medieval Latin poet whose work *De Peanctu Naturae* he may have known directly, for more information on this mysterious theme. And at the root of the poem is an ancient puzzle; the relation of time (which, since it is associated with movement and matter, is at the root of change) and eternity. The prime Christian authority on this is the eleventh chapter of St. Augustine's *Confessions*, a tense, excited meditation on the theme which is in itself remarkable philosophical poetry. Other philosophers contributed to the antithesis of change and permanence, time and eternity, and so there developed a body of medieval commonplace on the subject. Spenser had already treated it from a different angle in the Garden of Adonis, and his answer, though arrived at by a validating poetic process, is in both places the same: Adonis, though 'subject to mortalitee/ Yet is eterne in mutabilitie,/ And by succession made perpetuall.' The answer of Boethius had been that 'all things rejoice to return agai n o their nature,' and that in the long run they do not change from their proper kinds—their seminary natures, as we might say, if we were thinking of the Garden of Adonis. Through change they reach the perfection potential in their natures; but their mutual alteration inevitably implies change and decay also. The two aspects of their existence are complementary; mutability is the servant of the eternal qualities of things.

Views of this kind may be found in various philosophical systems, and there is no knowing whether Spenser in one place or another intended to reflect a doctrine less general than the body of commonplace of which I have spoken. Nature may be the Platonic *anima mundi*, the generator of all created things; and the lines that describe the outbreak of flower and blossom about her may reflect this. She may also be related to the Venus of Book IV; or Spenser may have invented this beautiful figure out of Alanus. Similarly, we cannot be sure that he had no deeper-laid programme for Mutability. As the daughter of Titans she is a child of earth, and so of Matter, which, on the neoplatonist scheme which equates progressive degrees of material contamination of the spirit with distance from the One, constitutes evil. Certainly she is also a highly generalized concept: Spenser can call her not only Mutability but also Change and Alteration; and she is also the corruption of the world which arrived with the fall to make, in Milton's words, all kinds 'unimmortal'. And although she cannot be independent of the strong contemporary sense of the decay of the world—a conviction sometimes strongly contested, but rife in the poetry, drama and devotional works of the period—she also represents something in which Spenser evidently took delight. 'All change is sweete', he said in *Muiopotmos*; 'for all that moveth, doth in *Change* delight,' he writes at the very end of the poem. The beauty and variety of the physical world is evidently a consequence of mutability. Thus Mutability has good arguments, Jove by comparison merely huff-puffing; and Nature ends the argument only by means of mysterious answer.

This account may leave the student in some doubt as to the interpretation of particular passages in the poem. He is referred to the Variorum, and to Mr. Nelson's book. Mr. Nelson has a particularly valuable discussion of a characteristic mode of Spenser's imagination, which is well illustrated in these cantos. Spenser constructs his ultimate answers out of reconciled antinomies. 'The world is not . . . a battleground on which light and dark, good and evil, battle for supremacy. Rather it is at once both light and dark, good and evil. In it, Una's black stole is as necessary to her as the sunny brightness of her face . . . Venus is both the mistress of the fruitful Garden of Adonis and the Acrasia-like temptress portrayed in the tapestry of Malecasta's Castle Joyeous, Concord is flanked by Love and Hate, Osiris threatens the state and preserves it. These are not superficial paradoxes; indeed the whole structure of Spenser's moral philosophy and the poem he wrote to express it is based upon them' (p. 303).

The reconciliation of opposites, by means of which Spenser in these cantos brings Time and Eternity into a poetic but still intelligible relation, is made possible by the dream-like character of his narrative, its 'truly imaginative absence of all particular time and space'. Mr. Graham Hough's imaginative use of a modern theory of dreaming does no harm unless we forget that Spenser held firm to rational meanings. He wanted a poem in which Red Cross could be both sinner and Christ, and still have a direct relevance to the crisis in history he

was observing. He wanted to celebrate the changing colours and shapes
of the world without giving up a radical conviction that the human
soul belonged ultimately to the stillness of eternity. Whenever his
poem seems to come down firmly on the side of eternity, as when
Red Cross marries Una, or the Blatant Beast is captured, or Scudamour
is reunited with Amoret—truth and a sense of physical and moral variety,
which is the world's joy as well as the source of its decay, makes him
draw back; he postpones the consummation of Una's marriage, defers
the loves of Scudamour and Amoret, allows the Beast to escape.
Similarly in his view of history, Elizabeth the Empress had brought
England to a new felicity and the Church to an ancient purity; she
was Astraea and the Virgin; yet all about her the times were bad, the
world in decay. In the triumphant resolution of Book I the theme of
Book VII is already latent. Spenser looks at things under both their
eternal and their temporal aspects; and in the last surviving part of his
poem he shows that he knows that must be a point at which he would
consider them together, allow them to confront each other. This makes
the Mutability cantos essential to our understanding of and pleasure
in the great poem as a whole.

VII, vii 3–27, 47–59; *viii.* 1–2

   2782. *agreed*: between Mutability and the Gods in canto vi.

   2783. Arlo: hill near Spenser's Kilcolman estate.

   2790. Pluto *and* Proserpina: king and queen of Hades.

   2810. *uncouth*: unknown.

   2811. *agrized*: horrified. (The purpose is to emphasize her beauty
and terror alike.)

   2820. *sheene*: beautiful.

   2824. Thabor: Mount Tabor, supposedly the scene of Christ's
transfiguration.

   2827. *equall*: level-topped.

   2838. Dan Geffrey: Chaucer.

   2840. Foules parley: *Parlement of Fowles*.

   2841. Alane: Alanus de Insulis, author of *De Planctu Naturae* (*Plaint
of kindes*) on whom see C. S. Lewis, *Allegory of Love*, pp. 98 ff.

   2848. *mores*: roots, plants.

   2854. Mole: forest near Kilcolman.

   2865. Hæmus: hill in Thessaly.

   2885. *tortious*: unjust, wrongful.

   2888. *equall*: impartial.

2890. *plaine*: complain.

2892. *challenge*: arrogate, claim.

2894. *heritage in Fee*: i.e. she possesses it by right of inheritance.

2901. *onely dew*: due only.

2908 ff. These stanzas are largely based on the teaching of Pythagoras in Ovid, *Met.* xv. 165 ff.

2908. *mauger*: in spite of.

2909. *regiment*: rule.

2911. *inholders*: tenants. *convent*: summon together.

2912. *incontinent*: immediately.

2921. *mortall crime*: Note the association between general mutability and the fall of man.

2923. *Prime*: spring.

2928. *beheasts*: commands.

2936. *on high . . . belowe*: See Genesis i. 7, which gave rise to endless speculation.

2937. *stil*: continually.

2944. *wights*: creatures.

2946. *plights*: conditions.

2950. *grange*: dwelling-place.

2951. *stead*: place.

2954. *middle meane*: medium.

2956. *spirit*: (monosyllabic).

2958. *tickle*: unstable, uncertain.

2959. *cleane*: completely.

2963. *chaunce*: happen.

2968. *pay*: i.e. inflict upon.

2980. *these fower*: i.e. the four elements, of which everything is constituted.

2983. *they*: i.e. the elements themselves.

2985. *sheere*: bright.

2992. *fire aethereall*: i.e. of the sphere of fire, between the earth and the moon.

2993. *usuall*: i.e. fire as we know it on earth, used in manufacture.

2994. Ops: goddess of the earth. Iuno: queen of heaven.

2997. *they*: i.e. the gods.

3018. *disseise*: dispossess, deprive.

3022. *vertue*: strength, influence.

3035. Cynthia: the moon. Spenser treats it as a planet, and proceeds to deal with the other six—Mercury, Venus, the sun, Mars, Saturn, and Jupiter, almost the order conventional under the Ptolemaic system, which was of course under challenge from others—notably the Copernican—at the time of writing.

3038. *crake*: boast.

3046. *far . . . order*: The Ptolemaic assumption that the planets had circular orbits had been progressively shaken by observations of their eccentricity; hence the profusion of ingenious hypotheses to save the old system. But Mercury was hard to observe, being too close to the sun, and in the Proem to Book V Spenser confines his remarks on eccentricity to the sun, Mars, and Saturn. That Mercury was also eccentric in orbit was a comparatively recent discovery, and perhaps Spenser had caught up with it (the subject was of much interest in England at the time) between writing Book V and these cantos.

3060. *cranks . . . crookes*: alluding to the epicycles of the Ptolemaic hypothesis.

3071. *make*: argue.

3078. *opposition*: astrological expression: the relation of two planets when their longitude differs by 180 degrees. *obliquid*: oblique; a less direct interaction between the planets.

3079. *Spheares*: the orbits of the planets.

3080. *clerkes*: scholars. *faine*: imagine.

3083. *starrie skie*: the 'crystalline' sphere of the fixed stars, held to be immutable and pure.

3084. *Starres*: the 'fixed' stars were known to move. *Signes*: i.e. of the Zodiac.

3085. *it self*: i.e. the crystalline sphere. Ptolemy said that 'inasmuch as the stars maintain their relative distances we may justly call them fixed, yet inasmuch as the whole sphere to which they are nailed is in motion, the word "fixed" is but little appropriate'. *wizards*: astronomers.

3090. *by transverse*: haphazardly.

3091. *let*: hinder.

3095. *addoom*: adjudicate, award.

3103. *whether*: which.

3108. *wayd*: considered.

3117. *For . . . desire*: By your aspiration to subject everything to alteration you unwittingly seek your own change, i.e. if Mutability rules all, you will be mutable too.

3120. *whist*: silenced.

3121. *see*: seat, throne.

Canto viii

3124. *whyleare*: lately.

3125. *way*: consider.

3129. *tickle*: unstable.

3132. *Short*: i.e. which makes short.

3140. *God of Sabbaoth*: God of Hosts.

3141. *Sabaoth*: Spenser may mean 'grant me sight of the Lord on the last day', but much more probably he means 'Sabbath', in the sense of Eternity—the stillness that follows the tumult of the six days of history.